INSIDE THE
WHALE
AND OTHER ANIMALS

590

INSIDE THE
WHALE
AND OTHER ANIMALS

Illustrated by Ted Dewan
Written by Steve Parker

DORLING KINDERSLEY
London • New York • Stuttgart

A Dorling Kindersley Book

Project Editors *Scott Steedman*
Mina Patria
Art Editor *Nigel Hazle*
Production *Norina Bremner*
Managing Editor *Simon Adams*
Managing Art Editor *Peter Bailey*

First published in
Great Britain in 1992 by
Dorling Kindersley Limited
9 Henrietta Street
London WC2E 8PS
Reprinted 1993

A CIP catalogue record for this book
is available from the British Library

ISBN 0-86318-813-3

Colour reproduction by
Dot Gradations, Essex, England

Printed in Belgium
by Proost

TO MÉMÉ

NO ANIMALS WERE CUT UP
OR EVEN EMBARRASSED IN THE
PREPARATION OF THIS BOOK

CONTENTS

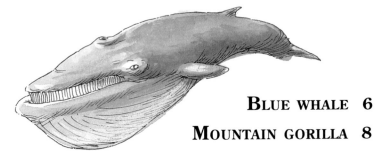

Introduction

As a curious and intelligent person, you probably wonder what goes on inside things. Maybe you've even taken apart a broken radio or an old watch, just to see what makes them tick. Animals are the ultimate machines, but looking inside one on the kitchen table could be a bit trickier – especially if that animal is a whale.

Each of our twenty-one animals is in some way special. Why no familiar creatures such as cats, dogs, and horses? Because they're all mammals, and their insides are fairly similar. We wanted to poke around in the corners of the animal kingdom, among the frogs and snails and spiders, to explore their fascinating, intricate, and, often beautiful anatomy.

All animals do the same basic things: breathe, eat, digest, get rid of wastes, sense the world, move about, and reproduce. But like vehicles on a motorway, from an electric minicar to a giant diesel lorry, each has something different under the bonnet. The rattlesnake can wrap its jaws around a victim bigger than its head, the bee has five hearts, and the octopus's throat goes through the middle of its brain. The starfish doesn't even have a brain, but it can spill its stomach out of its mouth. Each has come up with a very different design solution to the age-old problems of living.

For in nature, there's more than one way to skin a cat.

Ted Dewan

Steve Parker

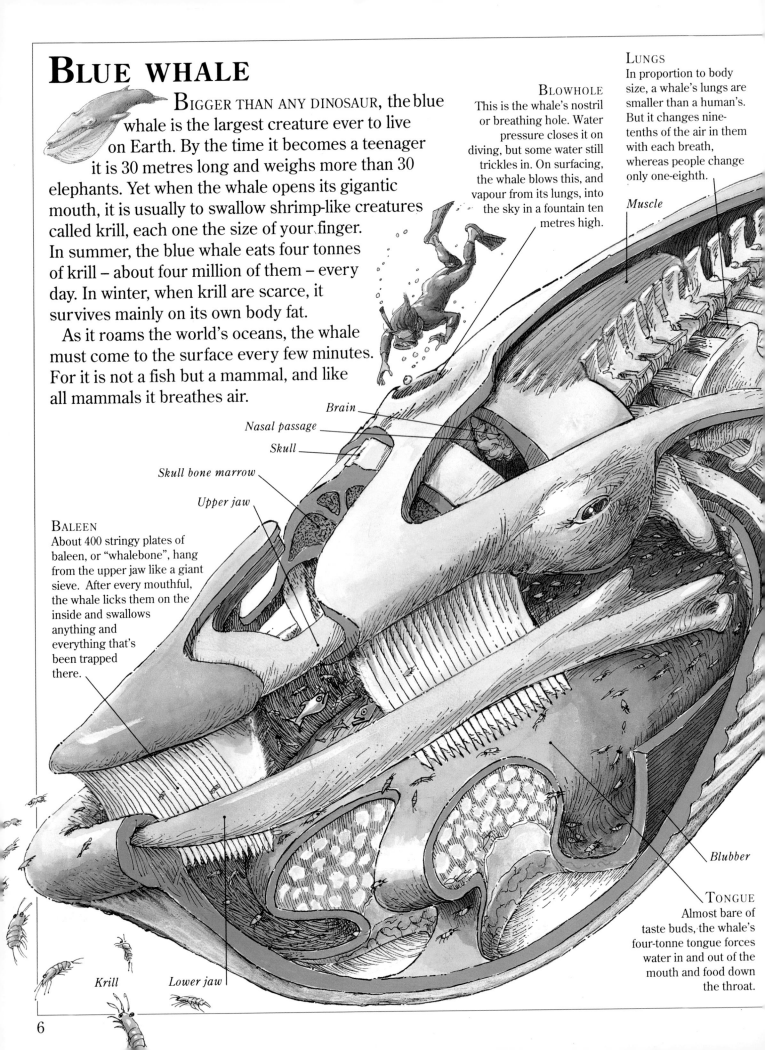

BLUE WHALE

BIGGER THAN ANY DINOSAUR, the blue whale is the largest creature ever to live on Earth. By the time it becomes a teenager it is 30 metres long and weighs more than 30 elephants. Yet when the whale opens its gigantic mouth, it is usually to swallow shrimp-like creatures called krill, each one the size of your finger. In summer, the blue whale eats four tonnes of krill – about four million of them – every day. In winter, when krill are scarce, it survives mainly on its own body fat.

As it roams the world's oceans, the whale must come to the surface every few minutes. For it is not a fish but a mammal, and like all mammals it breathes air.

LUNGS
In proportion to body size, a whale's lungs are smaller than a human's. But it changes nine-tenths of the air in them with each breath, whereas people change only one-eighth.

Muscle

BLOWHOLE
This is the whale's nostril or breathing hole. Water pressure closes it on diving, but some water still trickles in. On surfacing, the whale blows this, and vapour from its lungs, into the sky in a fountain ten metres high.

Brain

Nasal passage

Skull

Skull bone marrow

Upper jaw

BALEEN
About 400 stringy plates of baleen, or "whalebone", hang from the upper jaw like a giant sieve. After every mouthful, the whale licks them on the inside and swallows anything and everything that's been trapped there.

Blubber

TONGUE
Almost bare of taste buds, the whale's four-tonne tongue forces water in and out of the mouth and food down the throat.

Krill   *Lower jaw*

6

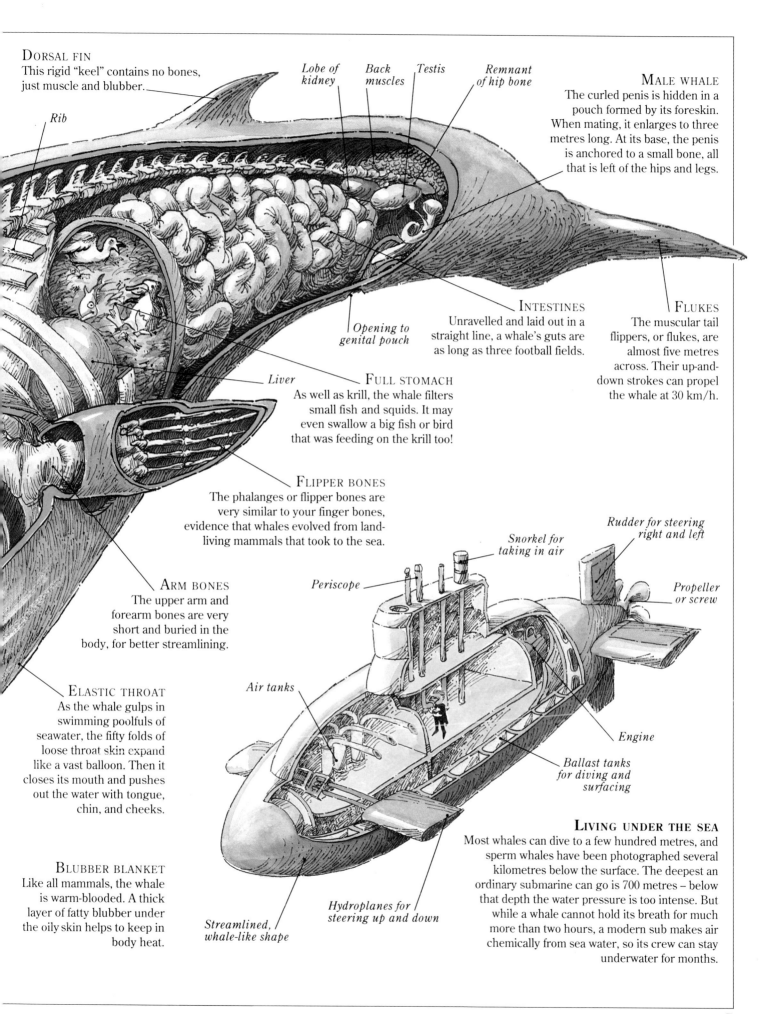

DORSAL FIN
This rigid "keel" contains no bones, just muscle and blubber.

Rib

Lobe of kidney

Back muscles

Testis

Remnant of hip bone

MALE WHALE
The curled penis is hidden in a pouch formed by its foreskin. When mating, it enlarges to three metres long. At its base, the penis is anchored to a small bone, all that is left of the hips and legs.

Opening to genital pouch

INTESTINES
Unravelled and laid out in a straight line, a whale's guts are as long as three football fields.

FLUKES
The muscular tail flippers, or flukes, are almost five metres across. Their up-and-down strokes can propel the whale at 30 km/h.

Liver

FULL STOMACH
As well as krill, the whale filters small fish and squids. It may even swallow a big fish or bird that was feeding on the krill too!

FLIPPER BONES
The phalanges or flipper bones are very similar to your finger bones, evidence that whales evolved from land-living mammals that took to the sea.

Rudder for steering right and left

Snorkel for taking in air

Periscope

Propeller or screw

ARM BONES
The upper arm and forearm bones are very short and buried in the body, for better streamlining.

Air tanks

Engine

ELASTIC THROAT
As the whale gulps in swimming poolfuls of seawater, the fifty folds of loose throat skin expand like a vast balloon. Then it closes its mouth and pushes out the water with tongue, chin, and cheeks.

Ballast tanks for diving and surfacing

LIVING UNDER THE SEA
Most whales can dive to a few hundred metres, and sperm whales have been photographed several kilometres below the surface. The deepest an ordinary submarine can go is 700 metres – below that depth the water pressure is too intense. But while a whale cannot hold its breath for much more than two hours, a modern sub makes air chemically from sea water, so its crew can stay underwater for months.

BLUBBER BLANKET
Like all mammals, the whale is warm-blooded. A thick layer of fatty blubber under the oily skin helps to keep in body heat.

Streamlined, whale-like shape

Hydroplanes for steering up and down

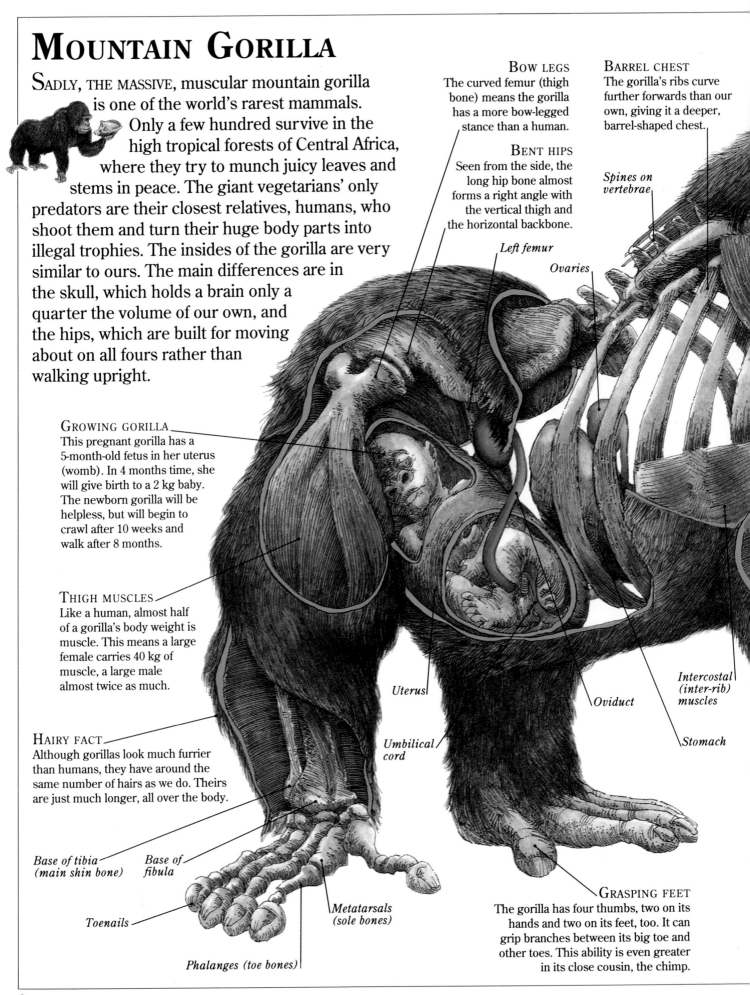

MOUNTAIN GORILLA

SADLY, THE MASSIVE, muscular mountain gorilla
is one of the world's rarest mammals.
Only a few hundred survive in the
high tropical forests of Central Africa,
where they try to munch juicy leaves and
stems in peace. The giant vegetarians' only
predators are their closest relatives, humans, who
shoot them and turn their huge body parts into
illegal trophies. The insides of the gorilla are very
similar to ours. The main differences are in
the skull, which holds a brain only a
quarter the volume of our own, and
the hips, which are built for moving
about on all fours rather than
walking upright.

BOW LEGS
The curved femur (thigh
bone) means the gorilla
has a more bow-legged
stance than a human.

BARREL CHEST
The gorilla's ribs curve
further forwards than our
own, giving it a deeper,
barrel-shaped chest.

BENT HIPS
Seen from the side, the
long hip bone almost
forms a right angle with
the vertical thigh and
the horizontal backbone.

*Spines on
vertebrae*

Left femur

Ovaries

GROWING GORILLA
This pregnant gorilla has a
5-month-old fetus in her uterus
(womb). In 4 months time, she
will give birth to a 2 kg baby.
The newborn gorilla will be
helpless, but will begin to
crawl after 10 weeks and
walk after 8 months.

THIGH MUSCLES
Like a human, almost half
of a gorilla's body weight is
muscle. This means a large
female carries 40 kg of
muscle, a large male
almost twice as much.

HAIRY FACT
Although gorillas look much furrier
than humans, they have around the
same number of hairs as we do. Theirs
are just much longer, all over the body.

*Intercostal
(inter-rib)
muscles*

Uterus

Oviduct

Stomach

*Umbilical
cord*

*Base of tibia
(main shin bone)*

*Base of
fibula*

Toenails

*Metatarsals
(sole bones)*

Phalanges (toe bones)

GRASPING FEET
The gorilla has four thumbs, two on its
hands and two on its feet, too. It can
grip branches between its big toe and
other toes. This ability is even greater
in its close cousin, the chimp.

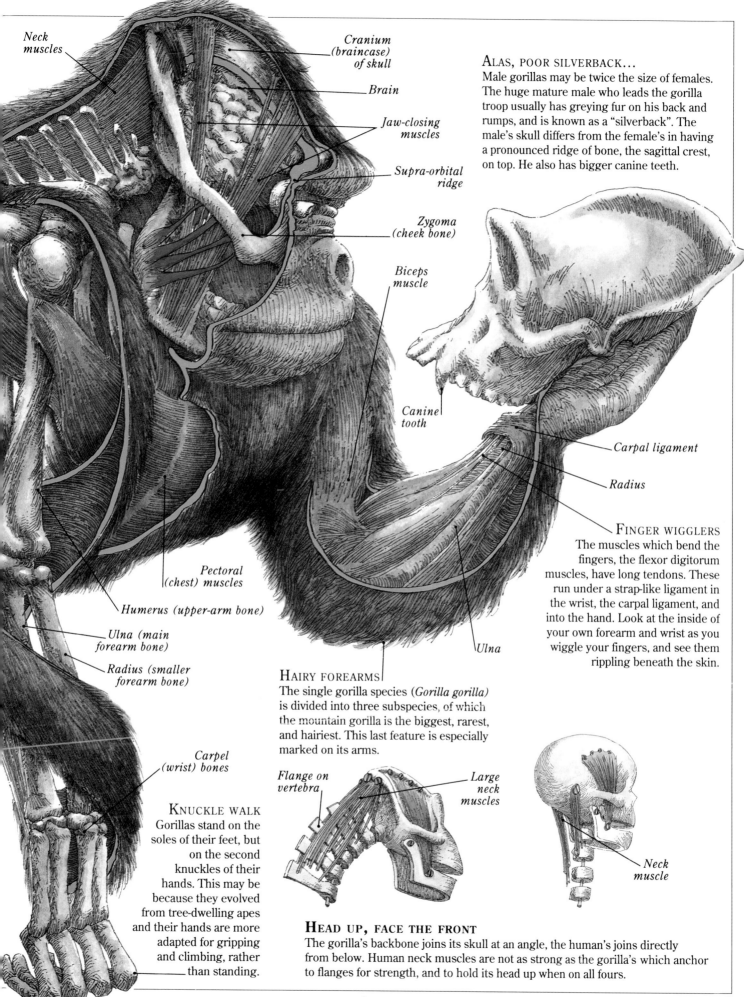

Neck
muscles

Cranium
(braincase)
of skull

Brain

Jaw-closing
muscles

Supra-orbital
ridge

Zygoma
(cheek bone)

Biceps
muscle

Canine
tooth

Pectoral
(chest) muscles

Humerus (upper-arm bone)

Ulna (main
forearm bone)

Radius (smaller
forearm bone)

Carpel
(wrist) bones

Carpal ligament

Radius

Ulna

ALAS, POOR SILVERBACK...
Male gorillas may be twice the size of females.
The huge mature male who leads the gorilla
troop usually has greying fur on his back and
rumps, and is known as a "silverback". The
male's skull differs from the female's in having
a pronounced ridge of bone, the sagittal crest,
on top. He also has bigger canine teeth.

FINGER WIGGLERS
The muscles which bend the
fingers, the flexor digitorum
muscles, have long tendons. These
run under a strap-like ligament in
the wrist, the carpal ligament, and
into the hand. Look at the inside of
your own forearm and wrist as you
wiggle your fingers, and see them
rippling beneath the skin.

HAIRY FOREARMS
The single gorilla species (*Gorilla gorilla*)
is divided into three subspecies, of which
the mountain gorilla is the biggest, rarest,
and hairiest. This last feature is especially
marked on its arms.

Flange on
vertebra

Large
neck
muscles

Neck
muscle

KNUCKLE WALK
Gorillas stand on the
soles of their feet, but
on the second
knuckles of their
hands. This may be
because they evolved
from tree-dwelling apes
and their hands are more
adapted for gripping
and climbing, rather
than standing.

HEAD UP, FACE THE FRONT
The gorilla's backbone joins its skull at an angle, the human's joins directly
from below. Human neck muscles are not as strong as the gorilla's which anchor
to flanges for strength, and to hold its head up when on all fours.

9

DROMEDARY CAMEL

ORIGINALLY DOMESTICATED FOR ITS MEAT, milk, and hair, the camel soon became a beast of burden, too. It has served people for around 5,000 years. Apart from the famous hump, the camel's insides are typically mammalian. It is the camel's overall shape and strange body chemistry that make it such a good traveller and desert survivor.

NECK VERTEBRAE
Like its close relatives, the llamas and alpacas, the camel has a long and very bendy neck, ideal for craning into trees and shrubs for food. It contains the standard seven cervical (neck) vertebrae found in all mammals, from mice to giraffes.

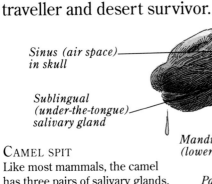

Sinus (air space) in skull

Long eyelashes

Sublingual (under-the-tongue) salivary gland

Parotid (near-the-ear) salivary gland

CAMEL SPIT
Like most mammals, the camel has three pairs of salivary glands. If threatened, it may spit its saliva with great force.

Mandible (lower jaw)

Palate (roof of mouth)

Oesophagus (gullet)

Submandibular (under-the-jaw) salivary gland

BLOWING BUBBLE
At the rear of the palate is a curious flap of skin known as the dulaa. In the mating season, the male spends a lot of time inflating his and blowing it out of his mouth, like a piece of bubble gum.

Throat

Trachea (windpipe)

FURRY INSULATION
Long, shaggy fur protects the camel from the scorching heat of the noonday sun and the often intense cold of the desert night. On hot days, the camel's body temperature can rise from 34 to 40°C before it starts to sweat. This saves precious water.

Woolly mat shades from sun

Extra fuel

Air filter

High clearance

WATER SUPPLY
The camel does not store water in its stomach. It survives droughts by producing very dry droppings, a small amount of urine, and by losing up to a quarter of its weight as water. When thirsty, it can drink up to 100 litres of water in a few minutes.

DESERT DESIGN
The "dune buggy", like the camel, is designed for travel in sandy, inhospitable areas. Wide tyres spread its weight to stop the vehicle from sinking, while a high clearance keeps the body up even when the going gets soft. Like the camel's hairy nostrils and long eyelashes, the air filter keeps windblown sand out of the engine. The extra fuel store allows long journeys.

Wide wheels

Wide-splayed foot

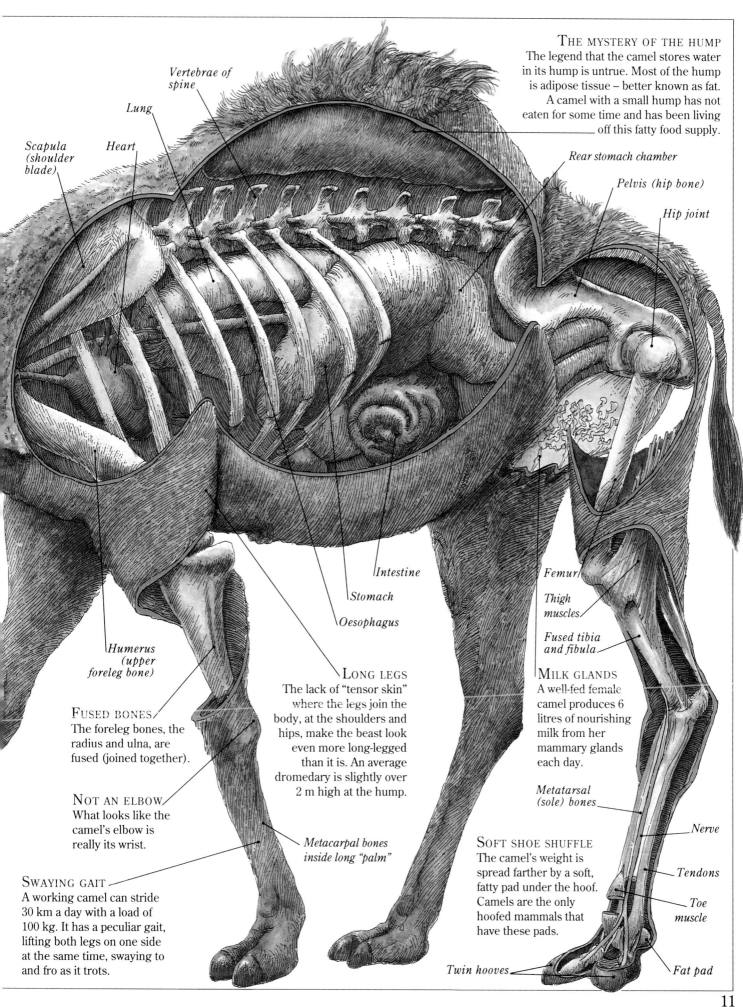

Vertebrae of
spine

Lung

Heart

Scapula
(shoulder
blade)

THE MYSTERY OF THE HUMP
The legend that the camel stores water
in its hump is untrue. Most of the hump
is adipose tissue – better known as fat.
A camel with a small hump has not
eaten for some time and has been living
off this fatty food supply.

Rear stomach chamber

Pelvis (hip bone)

Hip joint

Intestine

Stomach

Oesophagus

Femur

Thigh
muscles

Fused tibia
and fibula

Humerus
(upper
foreleg bone)

FUSED BONES
The foreleg bones, the
radius and ulna, are
fused (joined together).

NOT AN ELBOW
What looks like the
camel's elbow is
really its wrist.

SWAYING GAIT
A working camel can stride
30 km a day with a load of
100 kg. It has a peculiar gait,
lifting both legs on one side
at the same time, swaying to
and fro as it trots.

LONG LEGS
The lack of "tensor skin"
where the legs join the
body, at the shoulders and
hips, make the beast look
even more long-legged
than it is. An average
dromedary is slightly over
2 m high at the hump.

Metacarpal bones
inside long "palm"

MILK GLANDS
A well-fed female
camel produces 6
litres of nourishing
milk from her
mammary glands
each day.

Metatarsal
(sole) bones

Nerve

Tendons

Toe
muscle

SOFT SHOE SHUFFLE
The camel's weight is
spread farther by a soft,
fatty pad under the hoof.
Camels are the only
hoofed mammals that
have these pads.

Twin hooves

Fat pad

11

AFRICAN ELEPHANT

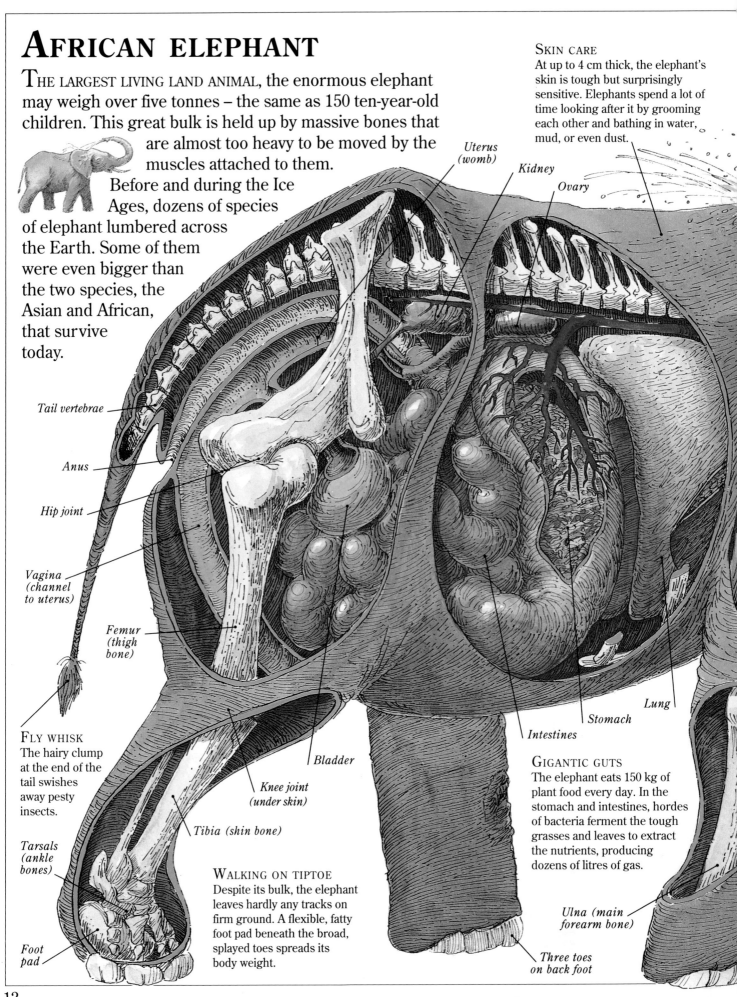

THE LARGEST LIVING LAND ANIMAL, the enormous elephant may weigh over five tonnes – the same as 150 ten-year-old children. This great bulk is held up by massive bones that are almost too heavy to be moved by the muscles attached to them. Before and during the Ice Ages, dozens of species of elephant lumbered across the Earth. Some of them were even bigger than the two species, the Asian and African, that survive today.

Tail vertebrae

Anus

Hip joint

Vagina
(channel
to uterus)

Femur
(thigh
bone)

FLY WHISK
The hairy clump at the end of the tail swishes away pesty insects.

Tarsals
(ankle
bones)

Foot
pad

Knee joint
(under skin)

Tibia (shin bone)

Bladder

WALKING ON TIPTOE
Despite its bulk, the elephant leaves hardly any tracks on firm ground. A flexible, fatty foot pad beneath the broad, splayed toes spreads its body weight.

SKIN CARE
At up to 4 cm thick, the elephant's skin is tough but surprisingly sensitive. Elephants spend a lot of time looking after it by grooming each other and bathing in water, mud, or even dust.

Uterus
(womb)

Kidney

Ovary

Lung

Stomach

Intestines

GIGANTIC GUTS
The elephant eats 150 kg of plant food every day. In the stomach and intestines, hordes of bacteria ferment the tough grasses and leaves to extract the nutrients, producing dozens of litres of gas.

Ulna (main
forearm bone)

Three toes
on back foot

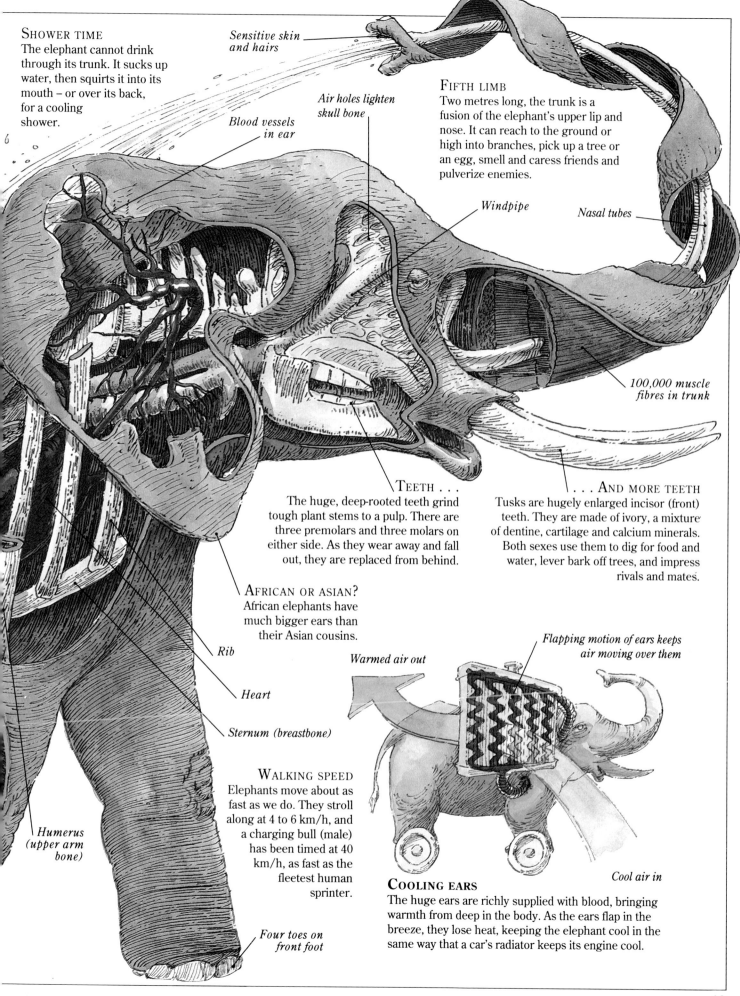

SHOWER TIME
The elephant cannot drink through its trunk. It sucks up water, then squirts it into its mouth – or over its back, for a cooling shower.

Sensitive skin and hairs

Blood vessels in ear

Air holes lighten skull bone

FIFTH LIMB
Two metres long, the trunk is a fusion of the elephant's upper lip and nose. It can reach to the ground or high into branches, pick up a tree or an egg, smell and caress friends and pulverize enemies.

Windpipe

Nasal tubes

100,000 muscle fibres in trunk

TEETH . . .
The huge, deep-rooted teeth grind tough plant stems to a pulp. There are three premolars and three molars on either side. As they wear away and fall out, they are replaced from behind.

. . . AND MORE TEETH
Tusks are hugely enlarged incisor (front) teeth. They are made of ivory, a mixture of dentine, cartilage and calcium minerals. Both sexes use them to dig for food and water, lever bark off trees, and impress rivals and mates.

AFRICAN OR ASIAN?
African elephants have much bigger ears than their Asian cousins.

Rib

Heart

Sternum (breastbone)

Warmed air out

Flapping motion of ears keeps air moving over them

WALKING SPEED
Elephants move about as fast as we do. They stroll along at 4 to 6 km/h, and a charging bull (male) has been timed at 40 km/h, as fast as the fleetest human sprinter.

Humerus (upper arm bone)

Four toes on front foot

COOLING EARS
The huge ears are richly supplied with blood, bringing warmth from deep in the body. As the ears flap in the breeze, they lose heat, keeping the elephant cool in the same way that a car's radiator keeps its engine cool.

Cool air in

BROWN BAT

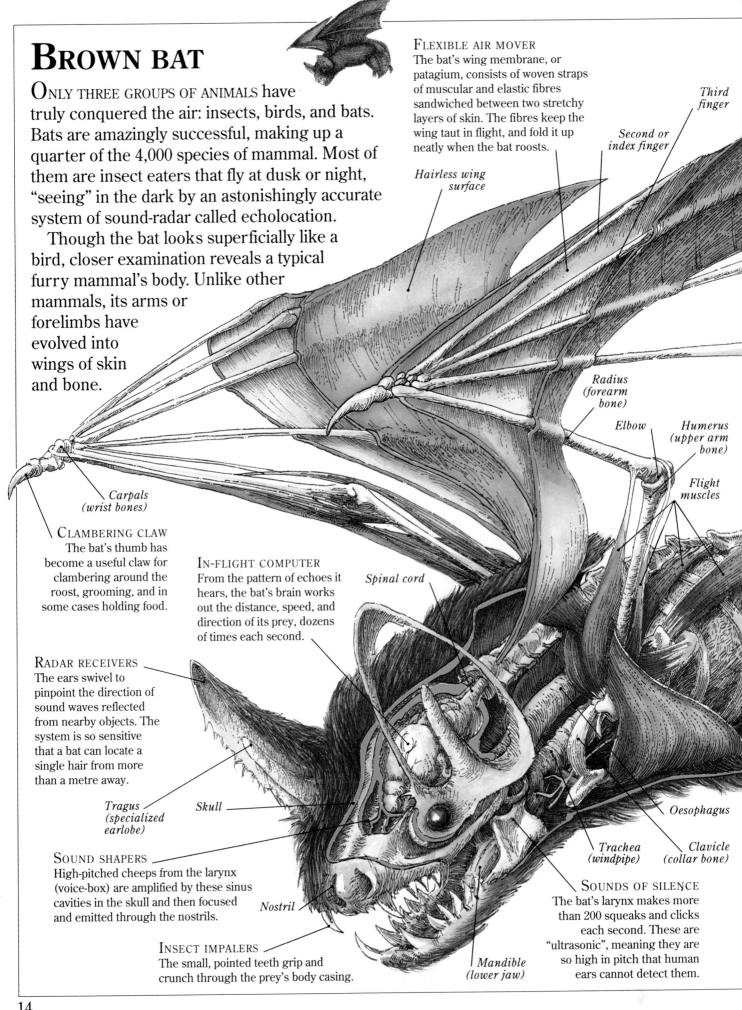

ONLY THREE GROUPS OF ANIMALS have truly conquered the air: insects, birds, and bats. Bats are amazingly successful, making up a quarter of the 4,000 species of mammal. Most of them are insect eaters that fly at dusk or night, "seeing" in the dark by an astonishingly accurate system of sound-radar called echolocation.

Though the bat looks superficially like a bird, closer examination reveals a typical furry mammal's body. Unlike other mammals, its arms or forelimbs have evolved into wings of skin and bone.

FLEXIBLE AIR MOVER
The bat's wing membrane, or patagium, consists of woven straps of muscular and elastic fibres sandwiched between two stretchy layers of skin. The fibres keep the wing taut in flight, and fold it up neatly when the bat roosts.

Hairless wing surface

Third finger

Second or index finger

Radius (forearm bone)

Elbow

Humerus (upper arm bone)

Flight muscles

Carpals (wrist bones)

CLAMBERING CLAW
The bat's thumb has become a useful claw for clambering around the roost, grooming, and in some cases holding food.

IN-FLIGHT COMPUTER
From the pattern of echoes it hears, the bat's brain works out the distance, speed, and direction of its prey, dozens of times each second.

Spinal cord

RADAR RECEIVERS
The ears swivel to pinpoint the direction of sound waves reflected from nearby objects. The system is so sensitive that a bat can locate a single hair from more than a metre away.

Tragus (specialized earlobe)

Skull

Oesophagus

SOUND SHAPERS
High-pitched cheeps from the larynx (voice-box) are amplified by these sinus cavities in the skull and then focused and emitted through the nostrils.

Nostril

Trachea (windpipe)

Clavicle (collar bone)

SOUNDS OF SILENCE
The bat's larynx makes more than 200 squeaks and clicks each second. These are "ultrasonic", meaning they are so high in pitch that human ears cannot detect them.

INSECT IMPALERS
The small, pointed teeth grip and crunch through the prey's body casing.

Mandible (lower jaw)

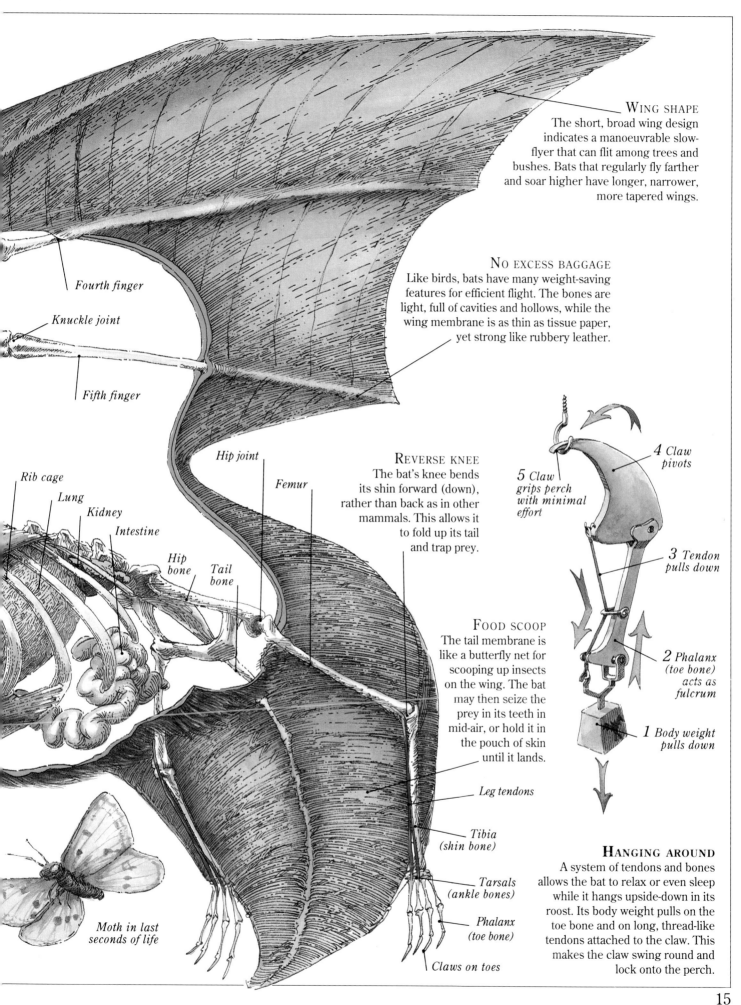

WING SHAPE
The short, broad wing design indicates a manoeuvrable slow-flyer that can flit among trees and bushes. Bats that regularly fly farther and soar higher have longer, narrower, more tapered wings.

NO EXCESS BAGGAGE
Like birds, bats have many weight-saving features for efficient flight. The bones are light, full of cavities and hollows, while the wing membrane is as thin as tissue paper, yet strong like rubbery leather.

Fourth finger

Knuckle joint

Fifth finger

Rib cage

Lung

Kidney

Intestine

Hip joint

Hip bone

Tail bone

Femur

REVERSE KNEE
The bat's knee bends its shin forward (down), rather than back as in other mammals. This allows it to fold up its tail and trap prey.

5 Claw grips perch with minimal effort

4 Claw pivots

3 Tendon pulls down

2 Phalanx (toe bone) acts as fulcrum

1 Body weight pulls down

FOOD SCOOP
The tail membrane is like a butterfly net for scooping up insects on the wing. The bat may then seize the prey in its teeth in mid-air, or hold it in the pouch of skin until it lands.

Leg tendons

Tibia (shin bone)

Tarsals (ankle bones)

Phalanx (toe bone)

Claws on toes

Moth in last seconds of life

HANGING AROUND
A system of tendons and bones allows the bat to relax or even sleep while it hangs upside-down in its roost. Its body weight pulls on the toe bone and on long, thread-like tendons attached to the claw. This makes the claw swing round and lock onto the perch.

GREY KANGAROO

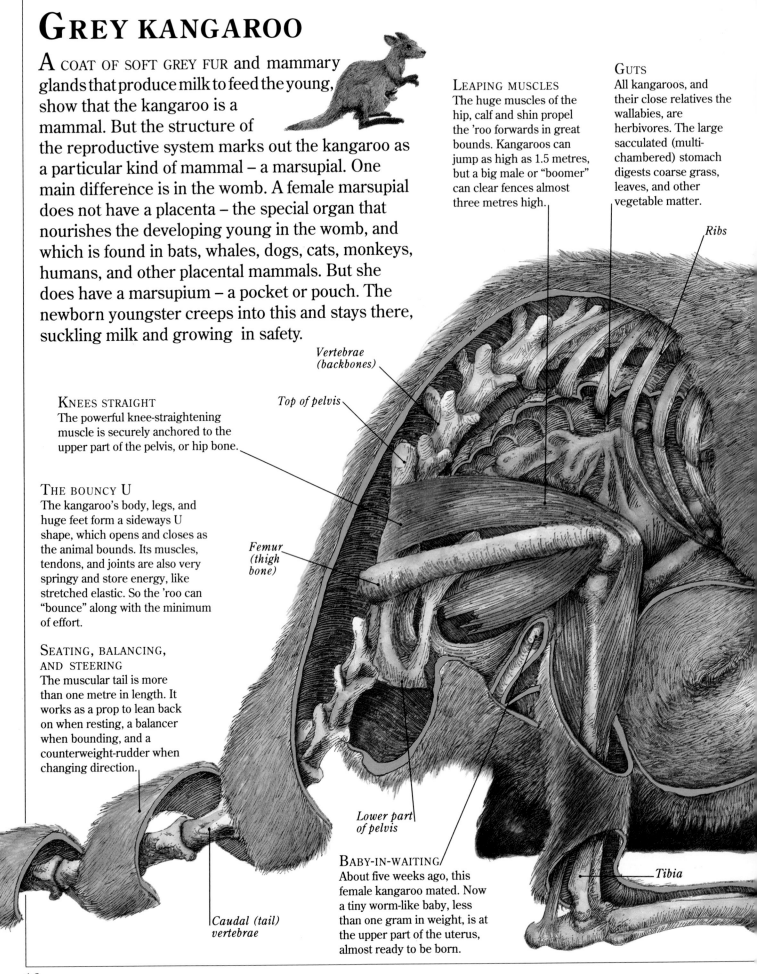

A COAT OF SOFT GREY FUR and mammary glands that produce milk to feed the young, show that the kangaroo is a mammal. But the structure of the reproductive system marks out the kangaroo as a particular kind of mammal – a marsupial. One main difference is in the womb. A female marsupial does not have a placenta – the special organ that nourishes the developing young in the womb, and which is found in bats, whales, dogs, cats, monkeys, humans, and other placental mammals. But she does have a marsupium – a pocket or pouch. The newborn youngster creeps into this and stays there, suckling milk and growing in safety.

LEAPING MUSCLES
The huge muscles of the hip, calf and shin propel the 'roo forwards in great bounds. Kangaroos can jump as high as 1.5 metres, but a big male or "boomer" can clear fences almost three metres high.

GUTS
All kangaroos, and their close relatives the wallabies, are herbivores. The large sacculated (multi-chambered) stomach digests coarse grass, leaves, and other vegetable matter.

Ribs

Vertebrae (backbones)

Top of pelvis

KNEES STRAIGHT
The powerful knee-straightening muscle is securely anchored to the upper part of the pelvis, or hip bone.

THE BOUNCY U
The kangaroo's body, legs, and huge feet form a sideways U shape, which opens and closes as the animal bounds. Its muscles, tendons, and joints are also very springy and store energy, like stretched elastic. So the 'roo can "bounce" along with the minimum of effort.

Femur (thigh bone)

SEATING, BALANCING, AND STEERING
The muscular tail is more than one metre in length. It works as a prop to lean back on when resting, a balancer when bounding, and a counterweight-rudder when changing direction.

Lower part of pelvis

BABY-IN-WAITING
About five weeks ago, this female kangaroo mated. Now a tiny worm-like baby, less than one gram in weight, is at the upper part of the uterus, almost ready to be born.

Caudal (tail) vertebrae

Tibia

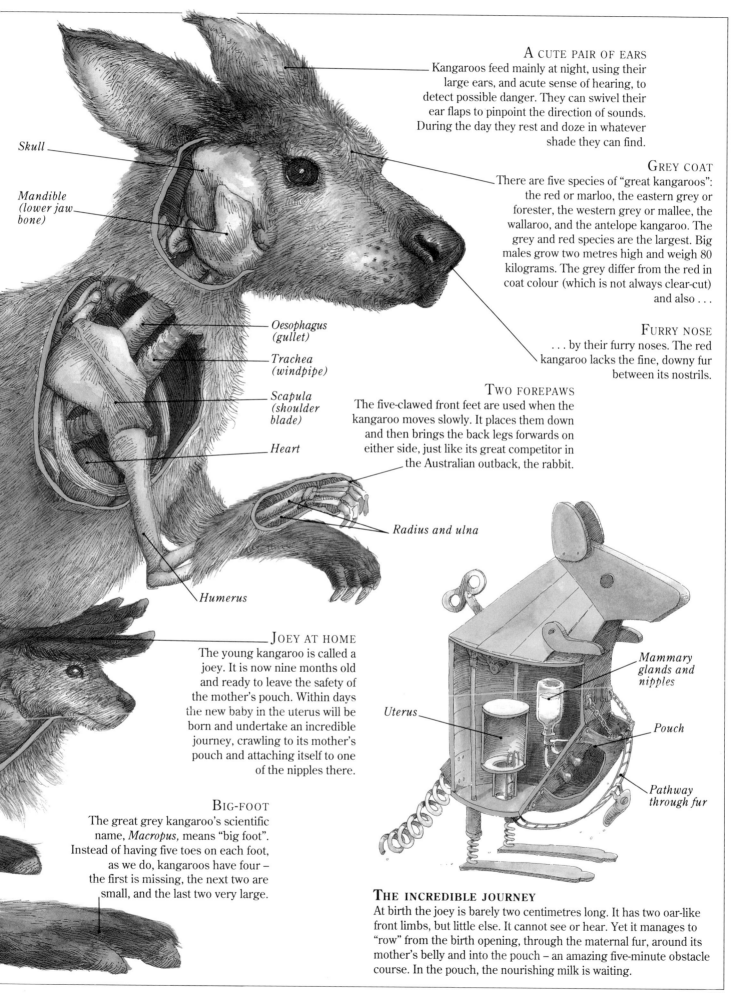

A CUTE PAIR OF EARS
Kangaroos feed mainly at night, using their large ears, and acute sense of hearing, to detect possible danger. They can swivel their ear flaps to pinpoint the direction of sounds. During the day they rest and doze in whatever shade they can find.

GREY COAT
There are five species of "great kangaroos": the red or marloo, the eastern grey or forester, the western grey or mallee, the wallaroo, and the antelope kangaroo. The grey and red species are the largest. Big males grow two metres high and weigh 80 kilograms. The grey differ from the red in coat colour (which is not always clear-cut) and also . . .

FURRY NOSE
. . . by their furry noses. The red kangaroo lacks the fine, downy fur between its nostrils.

TWO FOREPAWS
The five-clawed front feet are used when the kangaroo moves slowly. It places them down and then brings the back legs forwards on either side, just like its great competitor in the Australian outback, the rabbit.

Skull

Mandible (lower jaw bone)

Oesophagus (gullet)

Trachea (windpipe)

Scapula (shoulder blade)

Heart

Radius and ulna

Humerus

JOEY AT HOME
The young kangaroo is called a joey. It is now nine months old and ready to leave the safety of the mother's pouch. Within days the new baby in the uterus will be born and undertake an incredible journey, crawling to its mother's pouch and attaching itself to one of the nipples there.

BIG-FOOT
The great grey kangaroo's scientific name, *Macropus,* means "big foot". Instead of having five toes on each foot, as we do, kangaroos have four – the first is missing, the next two are small, and the last two very large.

Mammary glands and nipples

Uterus

Pouch

Pathway through fur

THE INCREDIBLE JOURNEY
At birth the joey is barely two centimetres long. It has two oar-like front limbs, but little else. It cannot see or hear. Yet it manages to "row" from the birth opening, through the maternal fur, around its mother's belly and into the pouch – an amazing five-minute obstacle course. In the pouch, the nourishing milk is waiting.

EAGLE OWL

A YOUNG TAWNY OWL leaves its perch and swoops silently through the dusk, across the field towards a rustle in the bushes. Without warning a bigger shadow envelops it; great talons pierce its body, and huge wings haul it, dying, skywards. The tawny owl, itself a formidable predator, has fallen victim to the speed and power of an eagle owl. Both these owls have features typical of birds, such as hollow bones, and an extensive system of air spaces among the body organs. The air spaces save weight, and they also help the birds to breathe efficiently by creating a one-way flow of air through their lungs.

NIGHT-SIGHTS
Most owls are nocturnal and have huge eyes to gather as much light as possible. The fields of vision of the two eyes overlap considerably, giving binocular or 3-D sight (as in ourselves). This enables the owl to see depth and judge distance more accurately.

OFFSET EARS
The ear opening on one side of the owl's skull is slightly lower than the opening on the other side. This may help the owl to pinpoint the direction of sounds. The facial discs of feathers also channel sounds towards the ear openings.

FOUND BY SOUND, STRIKE BY SIGHT
A hungry owl listens intently for possible victims, and turns its head to equalize the sounds coming into each ear. It then looks straight at the prey, which it can eventually make out in the gloom with its light-sensitive eyes. Sight takes over as the owl dives and grabs its meal.

WHAT'S THIS EAR?
The "ears" are simply tufts of extra-long feathers. The real ears are on the sides of the head.

WING BONES
Each forelimb bone has its equivalent in a mammal or reptile. Evolution has reshaped them for flapping flight, not walking.

TOO BIG TO TURN
Owl eyes are such a tight fit in their sockets that they cannot swivel. So the owl must twist or nod its whole head to look around. Its cervical (neck) vertebrae are very flexible – the bird can rotate its head through 180° to look directly behind itself!

Thumb

Carpals (wrist)

Radius and ulna (forearm bones)

Elbow

Humerus (upper-arm bone)

Ear opening

Iris

Retina

Lens

Maxilla (upper jaw)

Mandible (lower jaw)

Trachea (windpipe)

Oesophagus (gullet)

Pectoral (flight) muscles

Offset ears

Both eyes face forwards

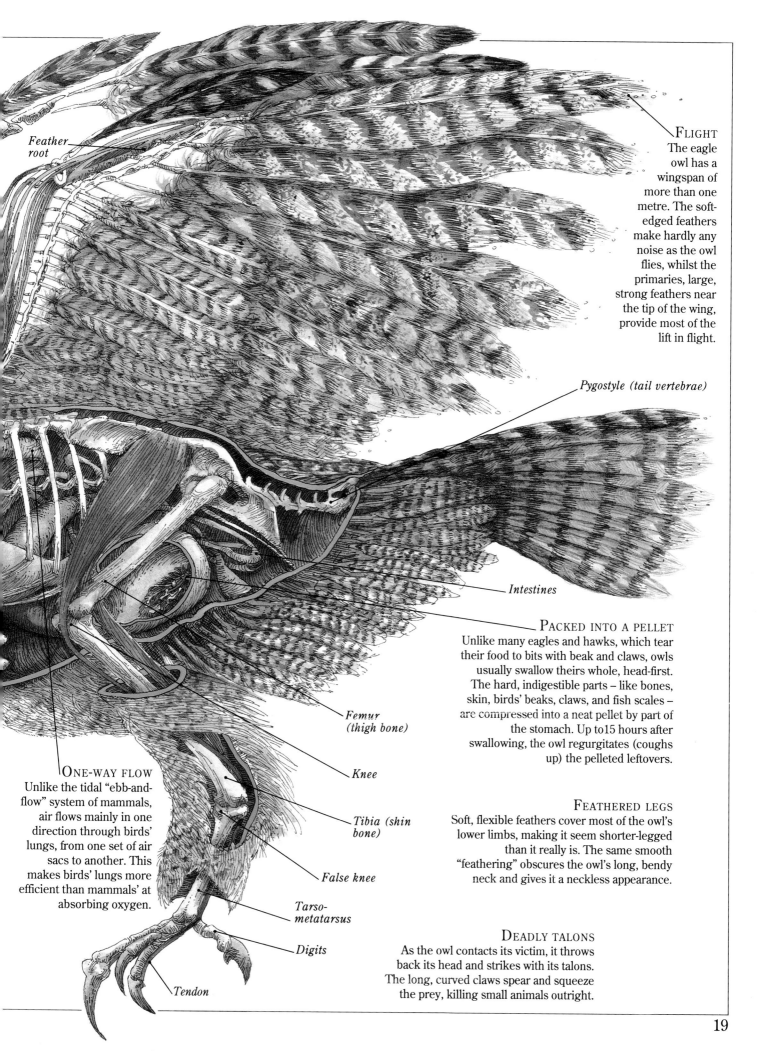

Feather root

FLIGHT
The eagle owl has a wingspan of more than one metre. The soft-edged feathers make hardly any noise as the owl flies, whilst the primaries, large, strong feathers near the tip of the wing, provide most of the lift in flight.

Pygostyle (tail vertebrae)

Intestines

PACKED INTO A PELLET
Unlike many eagles and hawks, which tear their food to bits with beak and claws, owls usually swallow theirs whole, head-first. The hard, indigestible parts – like bones, skin, birds' beaks, claws, and fish scales – are compressed into a neat pellet by part of the stomach. Up to 15 hours after swallowing, the owl regurgitates (coughs up) the pelleted leftovers.

Femur (thigh bone)

Knee

FEATHERED LEGS
Soft, flexible feathers cover most of the owl's lower limbs, making it seem shorter-legged than it really is. The same smooth "feathering" obscures the owl's long, bendy neck and gives it a neckless appearance.

ONE-WAY FLOW
Unlike the tidal "ebb-and-flow" system of mammals, air flows mainly in one direction through birds' lungs, from one set of air sacs to another. This makes birds' lungs more efficient than mammals' at absorbing oxygen.

Tibia (shin bone)

False knee

Tarso-metatarsus

Digits

DEADLY TALONS
As the owl contacts its victim, it throws back its head and strikes with its talons. The long, curved claws spear and squeeze the prey, killing small animals outright.

Tendon

19

CHICKEN

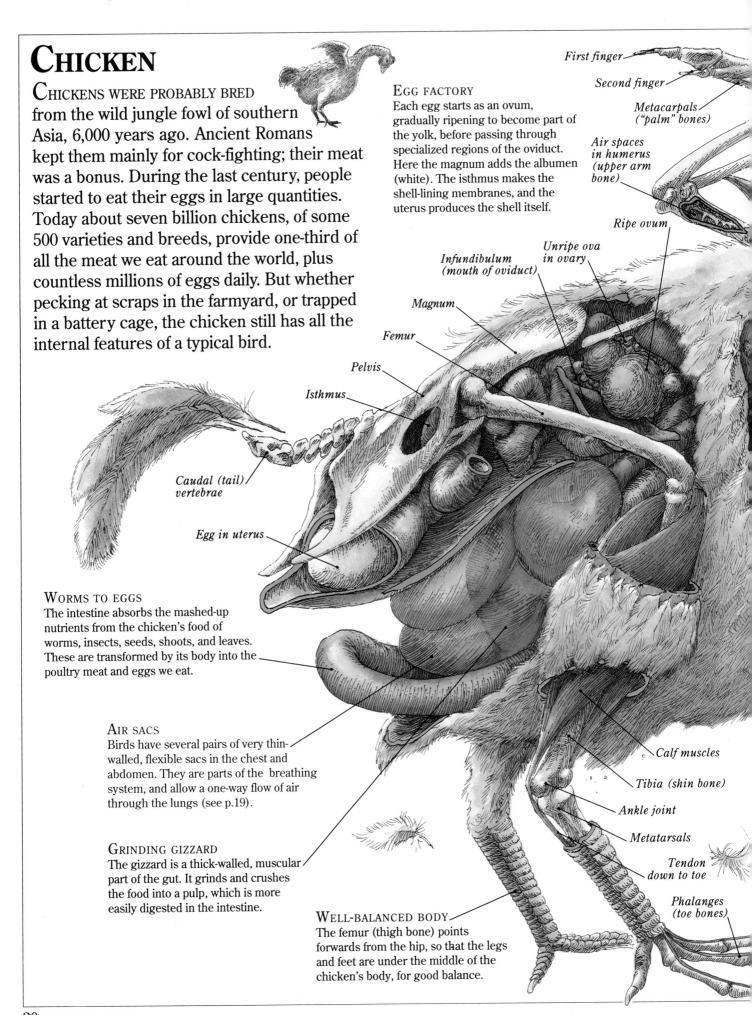

CHICKENS WERE PROBABLY BRED from the wild jungle fowl of southern Asia, 6,000 years ago. Ancient Romans kept them mainly for cock-fighting; their meat was a bonus. During the last century, people started to eat their eggs in large quantities. Today about seven billion chickens, of some 500 varieties and breeds, provide one-third of all the meat we eat around the world, plus countless millions of eggs daily. But whether pecking at scraps in the farmyard, or trapped in a battery cage, the chicken still has all the internal features of a typical bird.

EGG FACTORY
Each egg starts as an ovum, gradually ripening to become part of the yolk, before passing through specialized regions of the oviduct. Here the magnum adds the albumen (white). The isthmus makes the shell-lining membranes, and the uterus produces the shell itself.

WORMS TO EGGS
The intestine absorbs the mashed-up nutrients from the chicken's food of worms, insects, seeds, shoots, and leaves. These are transformed by its body into the poultry meat and eggs we eat.

AIR SACS
Birds have several pairs of very thin-walled, flexible sacs in the chest and abdomen. They are parts of the breathing system, and allow a one-way flow of air through the lungs (see p.19).

GRINDING GIZZARD
The gizzard is a thick-walled, muscular part of the gut. It grinds and crushes the food into a pulp, which is more easily digested in the intestine.

WELL-BALANCED BODY
The femur (thigh bone) points forwards from the hip, so that the legs and feet are under the middle of the chicken's body, for good balance.

First finger

Second finger

Metacarpals ("palm" bones)

Air spaces in humerus (upper arm bone)

Ripe ovum

Unripe ova in ovary

Infundibulum (mouth of oviduct)

Magnum

Femur

Pelvis

Isthmus

Caudal (tail) vertebrae

Egg in uterus

Calf muscles

Tibia (shin bone)

Ankle joint

Metatarsals

Tendon down to toe

Phalanges (toe bones)

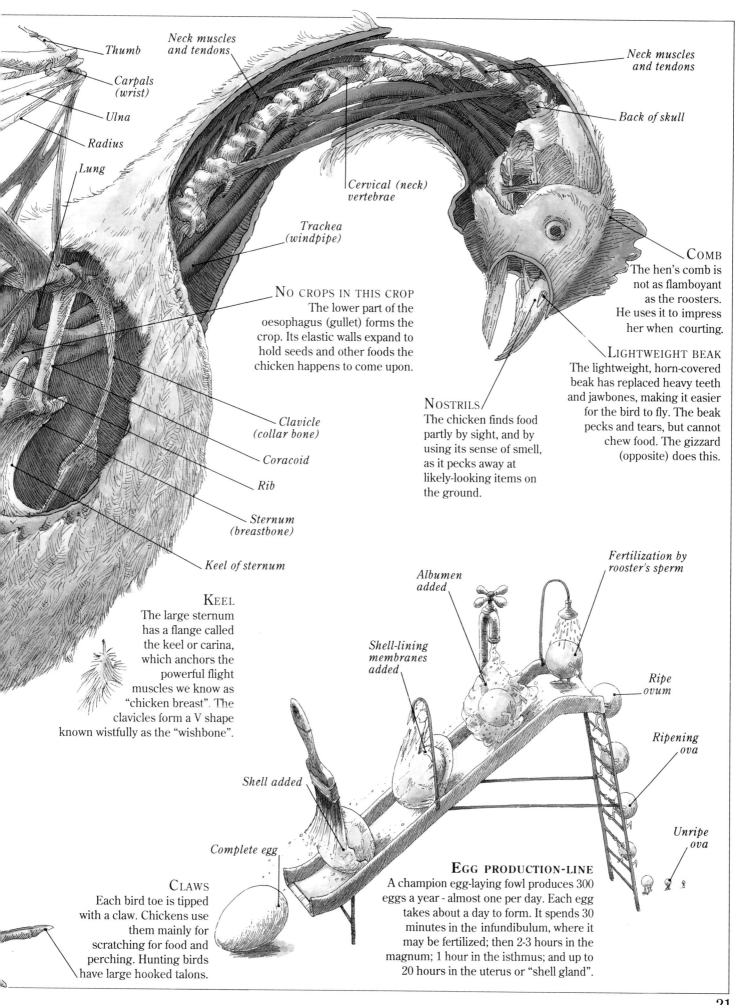

Thumb

Carpals (wrist)

Ulna

Radius

Lung

Neck muscles and tendons

Cervical (neck) vertebrae

Trachea (windpipe)

Neck muscles and tendons

Back of skull

COMB
The hen's comb is not as flamboyant as the roosters. He uses it to impress her when courting.

LIGHTWEIGHT BEAK
The lightweight, horn-covered beak has replaced heavy teeth and jawbones, making it easier for the bird to fly. The beak pecks and tears, but cannot chew food. The gizzard (opposite) does this.

NO CROPS IN THIS CROP
The lower part of the oesophagus (gullet) forms the crop. Its elastic walls expand to hold seeds and other foods the chicken happens to come upon.

NOSTRILS
The chicken finds food partly by sight, and by using its sense of smell, as it pecks away at likely-looking items on the ground.

Clavicle (collar bone)

Coracoid

Rib

Sternum (breastbone)

Keel of sternum

KEEL
The large sternum has a flange called the keel or carina, which anchors the powerful flight muscles we know as "chicken breast". The clavicles form a V shape known wistfully as the "wishbone".

Albumen added

Shell-lining membranes added

Fertilization by rooster's sperm

Ripe ovum

Ripening ova

Shell added

Complete egg

Unripe ova

CLAWS
Each bird toe is tipped with a claw. Chickens use them mainly for scratching for food and perching. Hunting birds have large hooked talons.

EGG PRODUCTION-LINE
A champion egg-laying fowl produces 300 eggs a year - almost one per day. Each egg takes about a day to form. It spends 30 minutes in the infundibulum, where it may be fertilized; then 2-3 hours in the magnum; 1 hour in the isthmus; and up to 20 hours in the uterus or "shell gland".

RATTLESNAKE

IN THE DRY BRUSH COUNTRY of North America, few sounds are more hair-raising than the harsh buzz of the diamondback rattlesnake. Under its scaly exterior this deadly snake has all the usual body parts of a land vertebrate – a skeleton, heart, intestines, liver – with a few additions, such as poison glands and nearly two hundred extra vertebrae. But to fit into the tubular body, some pairs of organs (such as the kidneys) are offset one behind the other, rather than being side by side. In other cases, one member of the organ pair (like the lungs) has shrunk, or even disappeared.

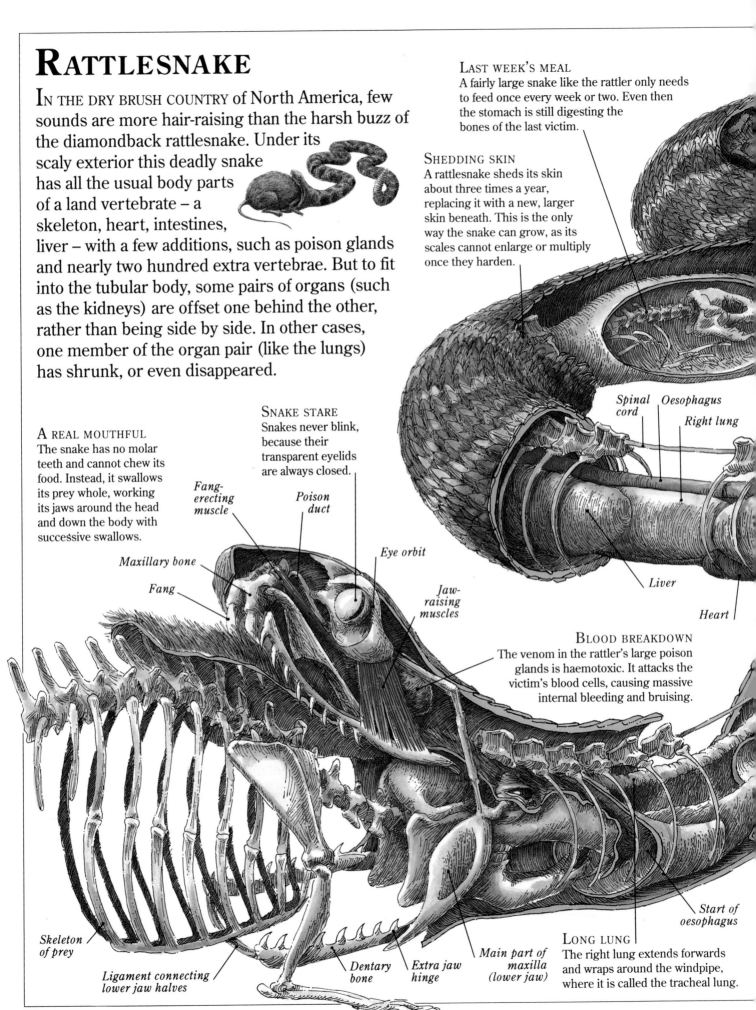

LAST WEEK'S MEAL
A fairly large snake like the rattler only needs to feed once every week or two. Even then the stomach is still digesting the bones of the last victim.

SHEDDING SKIN
A rattlesnake sheds its skin about three times a year, replacing it with a new, larger skin beneath. This is the only way the snake can grow, as its scales cannot enlarge or multiply once they harden.

Spinal cord

Oesophagus

Right lung

Liver

Heart

A REAL MOUTHFUL
The snake has no molar teeth and cannot chew its food. Instead, it swallows its prey whole, working its jaws around the head and down the body with successive swallows.

SNAKE STARE
Snakes never blink, because their transparent eyelids are always closed.

Fang-erecting muscle

Poison duct

Eye orbit

Jaw-raising muscles

Maxillary bone

Fang

BLOOD BREAKDOWN
The venom in the rattler's large poison glands is haemotoxic. It attacks the victim's blood cells, causing massive internal bleeding and bruising.

Skeleton of prey

Ligament connecting lower jaw halves

Dentary bone

Extra jaw hinge

Main part of maxilla (lower jaw)

Start of oesophagus

LONG LUNG
The right lung extends forwards and wraps around the windpipe, where it is called the tracheal lung.

22

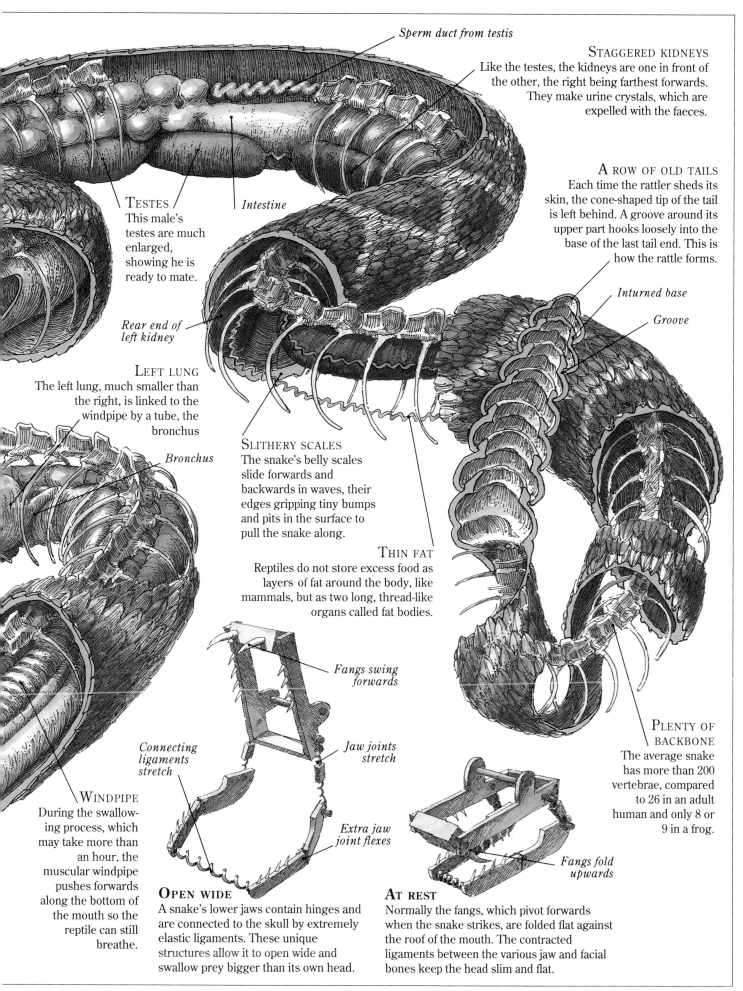

Sperm duct from testis

STAGGERED KIDNEYS
Like the testes, the kidneys are one in front of the other, the right being farthest forwards. They make urine crystals, which are expelled with the faeces.

A ROW OF OLD TAILS
Each time the rattler sheds its skin, the cone-shaped tip of the tail is left behind. A groove around its upper part hooks loosely into the base of the last tail end. This is how the rattle forms.

Inturned base

Groove

TESTES
This male's testes are much enlarged, showing he is ready to mate.

Intestine

Rear end of left kidney

LEFT LUNG
The left lung, much smaller than the right, is linked to the windpipe by a tube, the bronchus

Bronchus

SLITHERY SCALES
The snake's belly scales slide forwards and backwards in waves, their edges gripping tiny bumps and pits in the surface to pull the snake along.

THIN FAT
Reptiles do not store excess food as layers of fat around the body, like mammals, but as two long, thread-like organs called fat bodies.

Fangs swing forwards

PLENTY OF BACKBONE
The average snake has more than 200 vertebrae, compared to 26 in an adult human and only 8 or 9 in a frog.

Connecting ligaments stretch

Jaw joints stretch

Extra jaw joint flexes

WINDPIPE
During the swallowing process, which may take more than an hour, the muscular windpipe pushes forwards along the bottom of the mouth so the reptile can still breathe.

Fangs fold upwards

OPEN WIDE
A snake's lower jaws contain hinges and are connected to the skull by extremely elastic ligaments. These unique structures allow it to open wide and swallow prey bigger than its own head.

AT REST
Normally the fangs, which pivot forwards when the snake strikes, are folded flat against the roof of the mouth. The contracted ligaments between the various jaw and facial bones keep the head slim and flat.

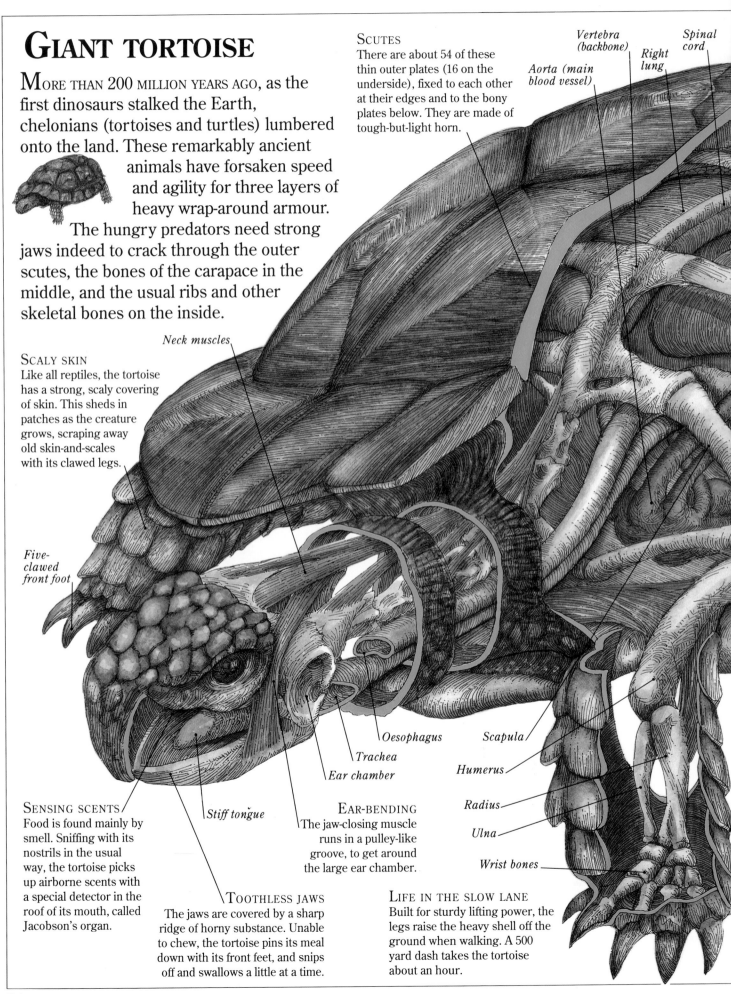

GIANT TORTOISE

MORE THAN 200 MILLION YEARS AGO, as the
first dinosaurs stalked the Earth,
chelonians (tortoises and turtles) lumbered
onto the land. These remarkably ancient
animals have forsaken speed
and agility for three layers of
heavy wrap-around armour.
The hungry predators need strong
jaws indeed to crack through the outer
scutes, the bones of the carapace in the
middle, and the usual ribs and other
skeletal bones on the inside.

SCALY SKIN
Like all reptiles, the tortoise
has a strong, scaly covering
of skin. This sheds in
patches as the creature
grows, scraping away
old skin-and-scales
with its clawed legs.

**Five-
clawed
front foot**

Neck muscles

SENSING SCENTS
Food is found mainly by
smell. Sniffing with its
nostrils in the usual
way, the tortoise picks
up airborne scents with
a special detector in the
roof of its mouth, called
Jacobson's organ.

Stiff tongue

TOOTHLESS JAWS
The jaws are covered by a sharp
ridge of horny substance. Unable
to chew, the tortoise pins its meal
down with its front feet, and snips
off and swallows a little at a time.

SCUTES
There are about 54 of these
thin outer plates (16 on the
underside), fixed to each other
at their edges and to the bony
plates below. They are made of
tough-but-light horn.

Oesophagus

Trachea

Ear chamber

EAR-BENDING
The jaw-closing muscle
runs in a pulley-like
groove, to get around
the large ear chamber.

LIFE IN THE SLOW LANE
Built for sturdy lifting power, the
legs raise the heavy shell off the
ground when walking. A 500
yard dash takes the tortoise
about an hour.

**Aorta (main
blood vessel)**

**Vertebra
(backbone)**

**Right
lung**

**Spinal
cord**

Scapula

Humerus

Radius

Ulna

Wrist bones

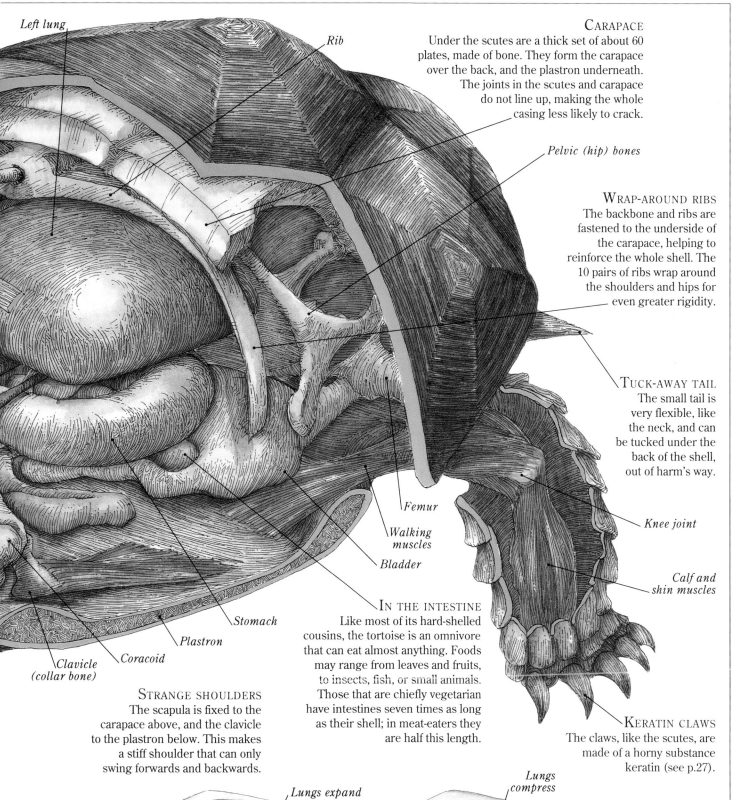

Left lung

Rib

CARAPACE
Under the scutes are a thick set of about 60 plates, made of bone. They form the carapace over the back, and the plastron underneath. The joints in the scutes and carapace do not line up, making the whole casing less likely to crack.

Pelvic (hip) bones

WRAP-AROUND RIBS
The backbone and ribs are fastened to the underside of the carapace, helping to reinforce the whole shell. The 10 pairs of ribs wrap around the shoulders and hips for even greater rigidity.

TUCK-AWAY TAIL
The small tail is very flexible, like the neck, and can be tucked under the back of the shell, out of harm's way.

Knee joint

Femur

Walking muscles

Bladder

Calf and shin muscles

IN THE INTESTINE
Like most of its hard-shelled cousins, the tortoise is an omnivore that can eat almost anything. Foods may range from leaves and fruits, to insects, fish, or small animals. Those that are chiefly vegetarian have intestines seven times as long as their shell; in meat-eaters they are half this length.

Stomach

Plastron

Coracoid

Clavicle (collar bone)

STRANGE SHOULDERS
The scapula is fixed to the carapace above, and the clavicle to the plastron below. This makes a stiff shoulder that can only swing forwards and backwards.

KERATIN CLAWS
The claws, like the scutes, are made of a horny substance keratin (see p.27).

BREATHING IN . . .
The rigid shell means a tortoise cannot expand its rib cage to breathe in. It uses muscles that push aside its intestines and other abdominal organs. These expand into the loose pockets of skin around the bases of the legs.

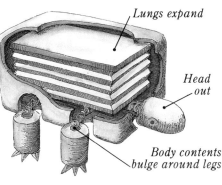

Lungs expand

Head out

Body contents bulge around legs

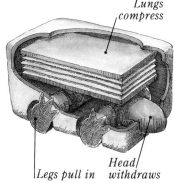

Lungs compress

Legs pull in

Head withdraws

. . . AND HOLD IT!
When the tortoise pulls into its shell, the legs squash its lungs and other organs – which means it can hardly breathe! Fortunately its body chemistry can cope with a build-up of waste carbon dioxide and lack of oxygen, so hiding doesn't mean suffocating!

NILE CROCODILE

A RELATIVE of those extinct giants, the dinosaurs, this toothy reptile looks like a primeval misfit in the modern world. In fact, the crocodile is one of nature's most successful designs, floating in wait in the River Nile today as it once did in the primordial swamp. Fossils show that its skeleton has barely changed over the past 200 million years, and paleontologists guess the same is true of its flesh and soft parts, which have left no remains. One reason for the croc's survival is the hard scales, which protect and camouflage it. Another is its huge mouth, built to rip chunks out of large prey or swallow smaller victims whole.

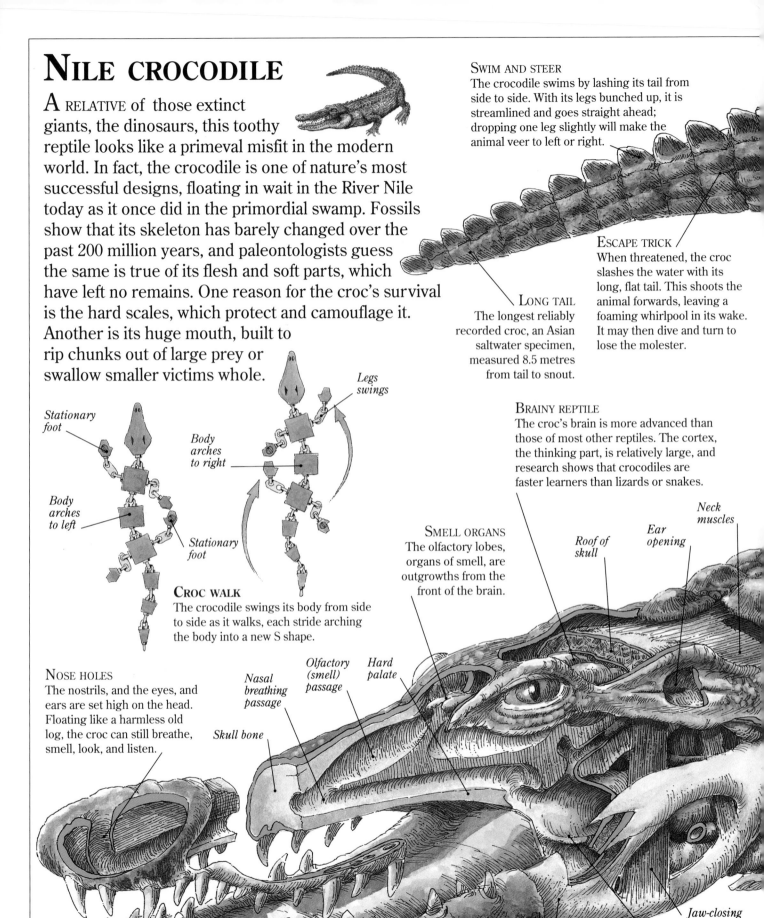

SWIM AND STEER
The crocodile swims by lashing its tail from side to side. With its legs bunched up, it is streamlined and goes straight ahead; dropping one leg slightly will make the animal veer to left or right.

LONG TAIL
The longest reliably recorded croc, an Asian saltwater specimen, measured 8.5 metres from tail to snout.

ESCAPE TRICK
When threatened, the croc slashes the water with its long, flat tail. This shoots the animal forwards, leaving a foaming whirlpool in its wake. It may then dive and turn to lose the molester.

BRAINY REPTILE
The croc's brain is more advanced than those of most other reptiles. The cortex, the thinking part, is relatively large, and research shows that crocodiles are faster learners than lizards or snakes.

SMELL ORGANS
The olfactory lobes, organs of smell, are outgrowths from the front of the brain.

Stationary foot

Body arches to left

Body arches to right

Legs swings

Stationary foot

CROC WALK
The crocodile swings its body from side to side as it walks, each stride arching the body into a new S shape.

Neck muscles

Ear opening

Roof of skull

NOSE HOLES
The nostrils, and the eyes, and ears are set high on the head. Floating like a harmless old log, the croc can still breathe, smell, look, and listen.

Nasal breathing passage

Olfactory (smell) passage

Hard palate

Skull bone

Jaw-closing muscle

Replacement tooth

Mature tooth

Maxilla (lower jaw)

THROAT VALVE
These flaps close on diving, so that the croc can eat when submerged without swallowing water.

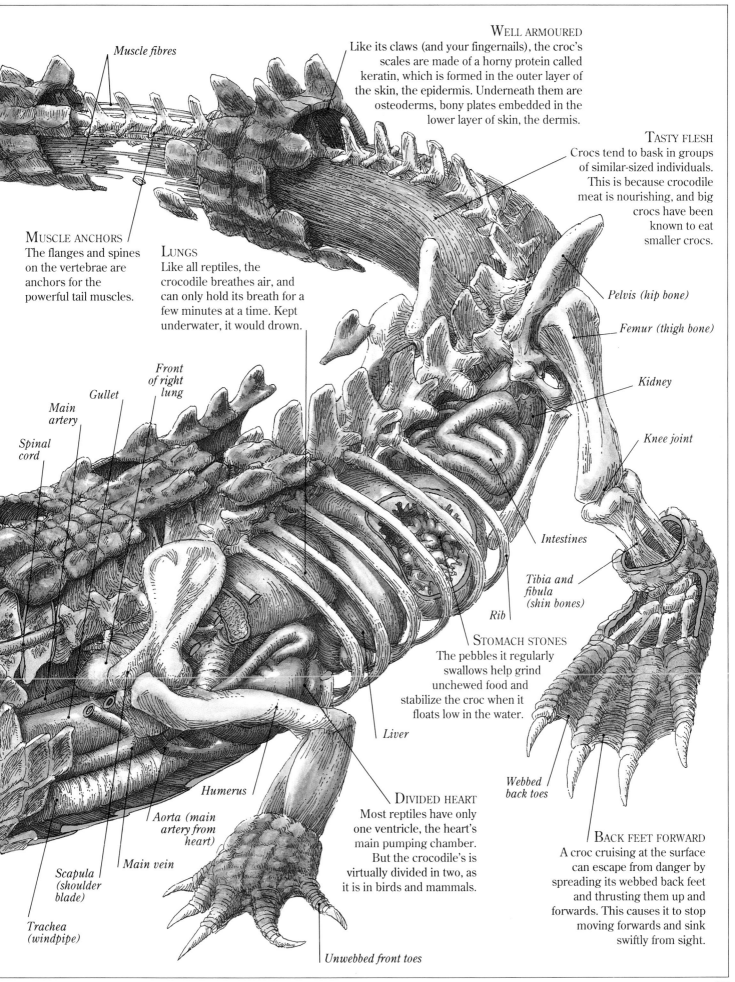

Muscle fibres

WELL ARMOURED
Like its claws (and your fingernails), the croc's scales are made of a horny protein called keratin, which is formed in the outer layer of the skin, the epidermis. Underneath them are osteoderms, bony plates embedded in the lower layer of skin, the dermis.

TASTY FLESH
Crocs tend to bask in groups of similar-sized individuals. This is because crocodile meat is nourishing, and big crocs have been known to eat smaller crocs.

MUSCLE ANCHORS
The flanges and spines on the vertebrae are anchors for the powerful tail muscles.

LUNGS
Like all reptiles, the crocodile breathes air, and can only hold its breath for a few minutes at a time. Kept underwater, it would drown.

Pelvis (hip bone)

Femur (thigh bone)

Front of right lung

Kidney

Gullet

Main artery

Spinal cord

Knee joint

Intestines

Tibia and fibula (shin bones)

Rib

STOMACH STONES
The pebbles it regularly swallows help grind unchewed food and stabilize the croc when it floats low in the water.

Liver

Humerus

Aorta (main artery from heart)

Main vein

Scapula (shoulder blade)

Trachea (windpipe)

DIVIDED HEART
Most reptiles have only one ventricle, the heart's main pumping chamber. But the crocodile's is virtually divided in two, as it is in birds and mammals.

Webbed back toes

BACK FEET FORWARD
A croc cruising at the surface can escape from danger by spreading its webbed back feet and thrusting them up and forwards. This causes it to stop moving forwards and sink swiftly from sight.

Unwebbed front toes

TRICERATOPS

THIS DINOSAUR DIED 65 MILLION YEARS AGO, so how do we know about its insides? Many well-preserved *Triceratops* bones from North America tell us about its skeleton. Its fossilized teeth and the preserved stomach contents of similar dinosaurs give clues to diet and digestion. Fossilized skin from other dinosaurs, and comparisons with living relatives like crocodiles, help to fill in other parts of the picture. But this reconstruction is still largely informed guesswork.

OL' THREE-HORNED FACE
The name *Triceratops* means "three-horned face", after the two large brow horns, and smaller nose horn. The dinosaur may have used these for defence, charging at molesters like a modern-day rhino. Or it could have locked horns with rivals while competing for the attention of mates.

BONY FRILL
The main structure of the frill was formed by backward projections from the parietal and squamosal, two bones of the skull.

WAVY EDGE
Small knobbly lumps of bone, the epoccipitals, gave the frill a wavy edge.

Pectoral girdle (shoulder bones)

Brow horns

NASAL FORAMEN
To save weight, the skull had various holes where firmness was less important.

Nose horn

Nostril

Trachea (windpipe)

Oesophagus (gullet)

Elbow joint

Radius

Jaw muscles

Ulna

SNIP-SNIP
An effective snipper for leafy vegetation, the parrot-like "beak" at the tip of the mouth was covered in a hard horny substance.

CUT-CUT
The rows of sharp teeth sliced and cut the vegetable food into smaller pieces.

CHEW-CHEW
A bar of bone at right angles to the main lower jaw, the coronoid process, gave extra anchorage to the strong jaw muscles, used for chewing food.

STUMPY LEGS
Massive legs like columns supported the creature's total weight of over five tonnes – the same as a large African elephant. Splayed toes spread this weight on the ground.

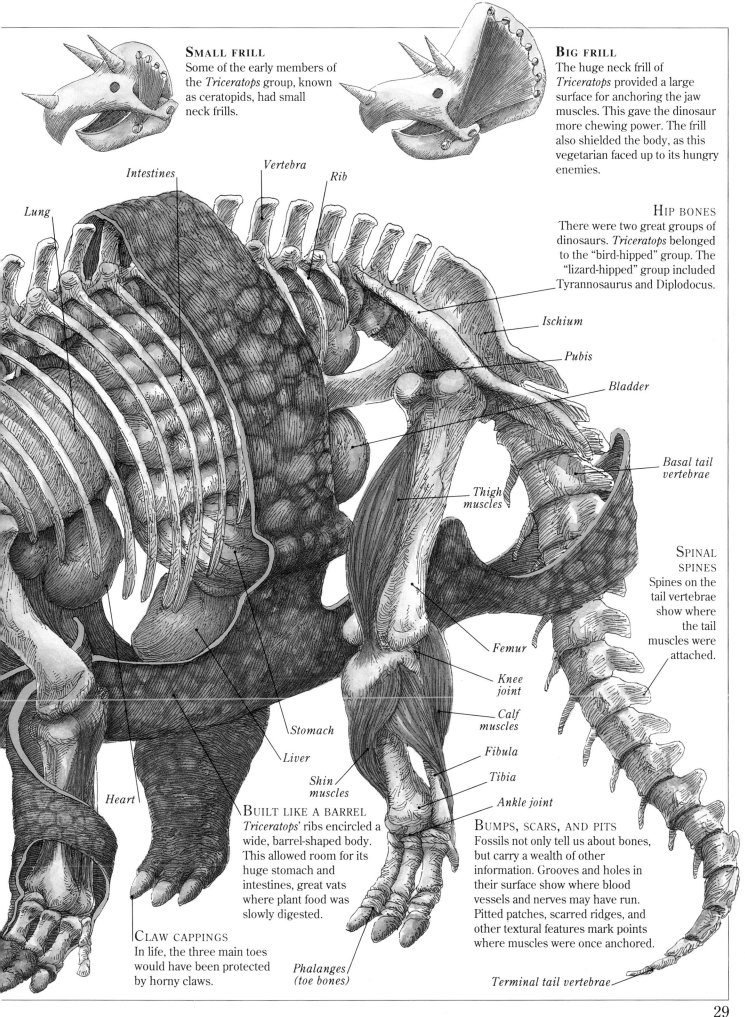

SMALL FRILL
Some of the early members of the *Triceratops* group, known as ceratopids, had small neck frills.

BIG FRILL
The huge neck frill of *Triceratops* provided a large surface for anchoring the jaw muscles. This gave the dinosaur more chewing power. The frill also shielded the body, as this vegetarian faced up to its hungry enemies.

Intestines

Vertebra

Rib

Lung

HIP BONES
There were two great groups of dinosaurs. *Triceratops* belonged to the "bird-hipped" group. The "lizard-hipped" group included Tyrannosaurus and Diplodocus.

Ischium

Pubis

Bladder

Basal tail vertebrae

Thigh muscles

SPINAL SPINES
Spines on the tail vertebrae show where the tail muscles were attached.

Femur

Knee joint

Calf muscles

Stomach

Liver

Fibula

Tibia

Ankle joint

Shin muscles

Heart

BUILT LIKE A BARREL
Triceratops' ribs encircled a wide, barrel-shaped body. This allowed room for its huge stomach and intestines, great vats where plant food was slowly digested.

BUMPS, SCARS, AND PITS
Fossils not only tell us about bones, but carry a wealth of other information. Grooves and holes in their surface show where blood vessels and nerves may have run. Pitted patches, scarred ridges, and other textural features mark points where muscles were once anchored.

CLAW CAPPINGS
In life, the three main toes would have been protected by horny claws.

Phalanges (toe bones)

Terminal tail vertebrae

GREEN FROG

HOME FOR THE TYPICAL FROG is quiet, cool, and damp. The frog is a predator, feeding on worms, beetles, flies, slugs, and similar small creatures. For most of the year, it lurks in the undergrowth, or some other shady place, waiting for food to wander by. But the frog is also an amphibian, and every year it returns to water to breed. Female frogs lay jelly-covered eggs, or spawn, that hatch into tadpoles. The frog has a bony backbone, skeleton, and four limbs. There are only nine or fewer vertebrae in the back-bone, and no obvious neck, or tail. The name for the frog group is *Anura*, meaning "tailless".

COMPACT DESIGN
Unlike its enormous legs, the frog's body is short, round, and compact. This reduces the risks of its spine and organs shaking, bending or twisting too much during a jump, and causing harm.

POISON
A frog's skin contains mucous glands, which make its slippery covering, to prevent too much water loss. It also has some poison glands, which ooze a vile-tasting fluid if the frog is attacked.

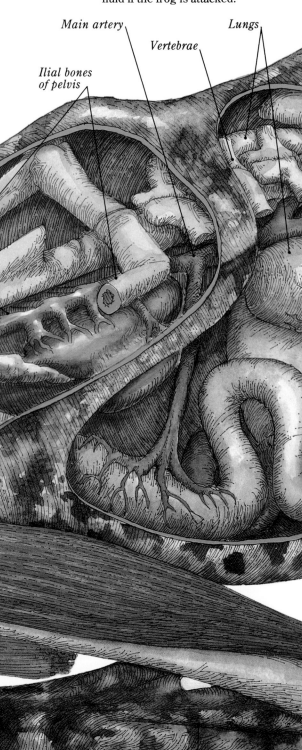

Main artery

Lungs

Vertebrae

Ilial bones of pelvis

Kidney

Urostyle

Anus

Ball and socket of hip

Femur

Tibia-fibula

Ankle joint

LIVING ELECTRICITY
In 1780, while working with leg muscles dissected from a dead frog, the Italian scientist, Luigi Galvani, saw that the muscles shortened when touched with certain metals. Later, in about 1800, this led to the invention of the electric battery, by Alessandro Volta.

Astragalus

Calcaneum

Webbing between digits

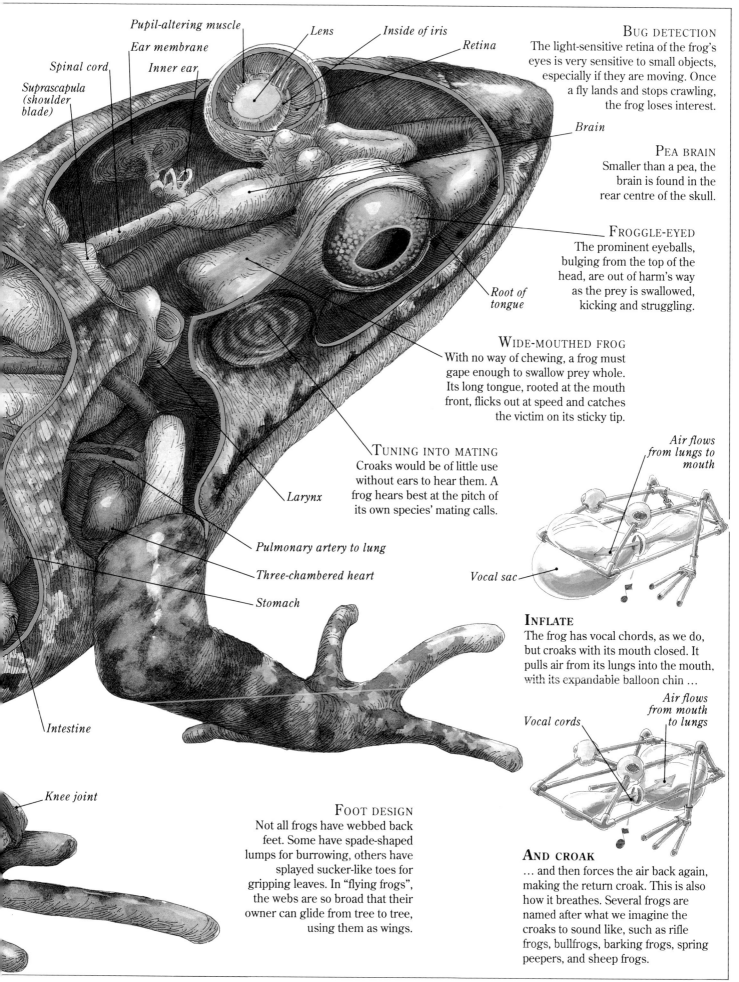

Pupil-altering muscle

Ear membrane

Spinal cord

Inner ear

Suprascapula (shoulder blade)

Lens

Inside of iris

Retina

BUG DETECTION
The light-sensitive retina of the frog's eyes is very sensitive to small objects, especially if they are moving. Once a fly lands and stops crawling, the frog loses interest.

Brain

PEA BRAIN
Smaller than a pea, the brain is found in the rear centre of the skull.

FROGGLE-EYED
The prominent eyeballs, bulging from the top of the head, are out of harm's way as the prey is swallowed, kicking and struggling.

Root of tongue

WIDE-MOUTHED FROG
With no way of chewing, a frog must gape enough to swallow prey whole. Its long tongue, rooted at the mouth front, flicks out at speed and catches the victim on its sticky tip.

TUNING INTO MATING
Croaks would be of little use without ears to hear them. A frog hears best at the pitch of its own species' mating calls.

Larynx

Pulmonary artery to lung

Three-chambered heart

Stomach

Intestine

Knee joint

Air flows from lungs to mouth

Vocal sac

INFLATE
The frog has vocal chords, as we do, but croaks with its mouth closed. It pulls air from its lungs into the mouth, with its expandable balloon chin …

Vocal cords

Air flows from mouth to lungs

AND CROAK
… and then forces the air back again, making the return croak. This is also how it breathes. Several frogs are named after what we imagine the croaks to sound like, such as rifle frogs, bullfrogs, barking frogs, spring peepers, and sheep frogs.

FOOT DESIGN
Not all frogs have webbed back feet. Some have spade-shaped lumps for burrowing, others have splayed sucker-like toes for gripping leaves. In "flying frogs", the webs are so broad that their owner can glide from tree to tree, using them as wings.

31

GREAT WHITE SHARK

NEVER QUITE AS BIG as it seems in the cinema, the great white is nonetheless a fearsome eating machine. At a mere six metres, it is still ten metres shorter than the largest fish, the whale shark. But while that monster eats nothing but tiny plankton, the great white is a carnivore that occasionally lives up to its reputation as a man-eater.

Sharks and their relatives, skates and rays, are chondrichthyes or "cartilage fishes". They differ from the more numerous osteichthyes, "bony fishes", chiefly in having a skeleton made of cartilage, not bone. Fossils show that the basic shark structure must be successful, as it has remained virtually unchanged for the last 300 million years.

SWIMMING FOR LIFE
Sharks lack the inflatable swim bladder that allows bony fish to control their buoyancy. Most sharks must swim endlessly. If they stop, they sink to the bottom, and may drown from a lack of water flowing over the gills.

Fin rays support fin

First dorsal fin

BACK "BONE"
The vertebrae, shaped like cottonreels and made of cartilage, may be strengthened with calcium minerals, as bone is. Inside are two tunnels down which run the spinal cord and the notocord, a primitive spinal column.

Main swimming muscles

Oesophagus

Kidney

Testis

Notocord

Spinal cord

UPTURNED SPINE
The spinal column bends up to support the upper, or superior, lobe of the caudal fin (the tail).

TOP-POWERFUL TAIL
Since its upper lobe is larger than its lower one, the tail's thrashing movements don't just drive the shark forwards – they also push its head down. This nosedive is countered by the fish's wedge-shaped head and its pectoral fins, which act like hydrofoils to lift the front end.

Second dorsal fin

Centrum (body) of vertebra

Rectal gland

RAYS FOR THE TAIL
The lower or inferior lobe of the tail is braced by long lower extensions of the vertebrae, called haemal rays.

Anal fin

Pelvic fin

Blood vessels to fin

SPERM JOURNEY
Sperm made in the testes pass along the Wolffian duct on the way to being stored and then expelled during mating.

ROTATING CLASPERS
The male shark has tube-shaped claspers developed from parts of his pelvic fin. During mating, he swivels these forward and inserts them into the female's cloaca (reproductive opening).

SANDPAPER SKIN
Notoriously rough and tough, shark skin is covered with placoid scales, like tiny teeth all pointing backwards.

PECTORAL FIN
The shark's propulsive power comes mainly from its tail. Its other fins are inflexible and it cannot "row" itself along with them, as can many bony fish.

32

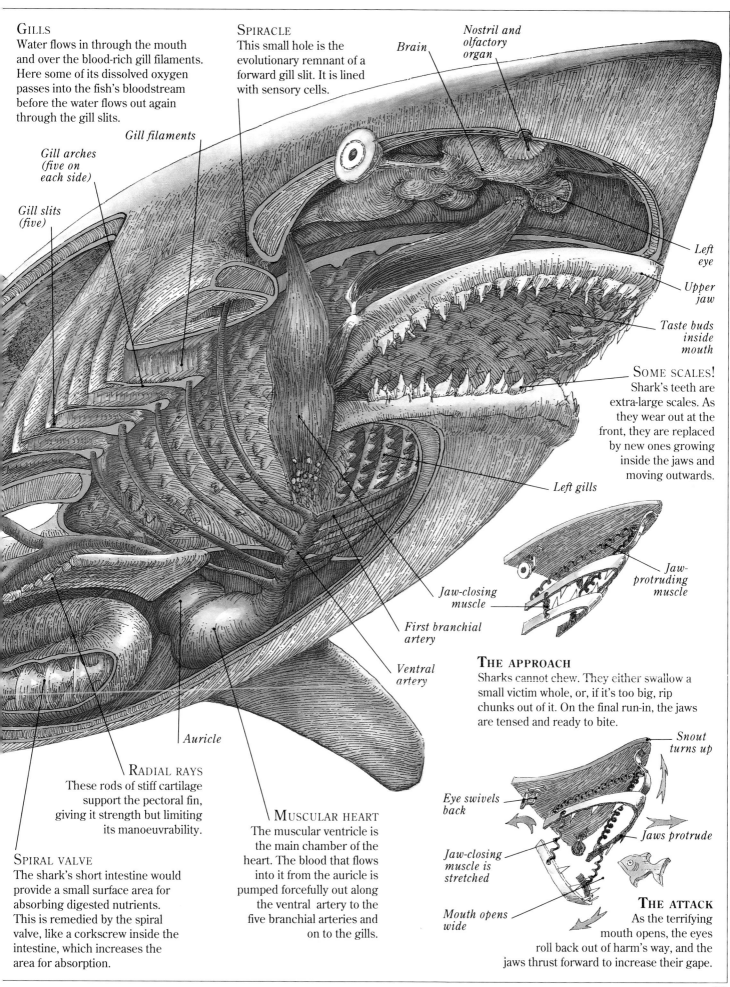

GILLS
Water flows in through the mouth and over the blood-rich gill filaments. Here some of its dissolved oxygen passes into the fish's bloodstream before the water flows out again through the gill slits.

Gill filaments

Gill arches (five on each side)

Gill slits (five)

SPIRACLE
This small hole is the evolutionary remnant of a forward gill slit. It is lined with sensory cells.

Brain

Nostril and olfactory organ

Left eye

Upper jaw

Taste buds inside mouth

SOME SCALES!
Shark's teeth are extra-large scales. As they wear out at the front, they are replaced by new ones growing inside the jaws and moving outwards.

Left gills

Jaw-closing muscle

First branchial artery

Ventral artery

Jaw-protruding muscle

THE APPROACH
Sharks cannot chew. They either swallow a small victim whole, or, if it's too big, rip chunks out of it. On the final run-in, the jaws are tensed and ready to bite.

Auricle

RADIAL RAYS
These rods of stiff cartilage support the pectoral fin, giving it strength but limiting its manoeuvrability.

SPIRAL VALVE
The shark's short intestine would provide a small surface area for absorbing digested nutrients. This is remedied by the spiral valve, like a corkscrew inside the intestine, which increases the area for absorption.

MUSCULAR HEART
The muscular ventricle is the main chamber of the heart. The blood that flows into it from the auricle is pumped forcefully out along the ventral artery to the five branchial arteries and on to the gills.

Snout turns up

Eye swivels back

Jaws protrude

Jaw-closing muscle is stretched

Mouth opens wide

THE ATTACK
As the terrifying mouth opens, the eyes roll back out of harm's way, and the jaws thrust forward to increase their gape.

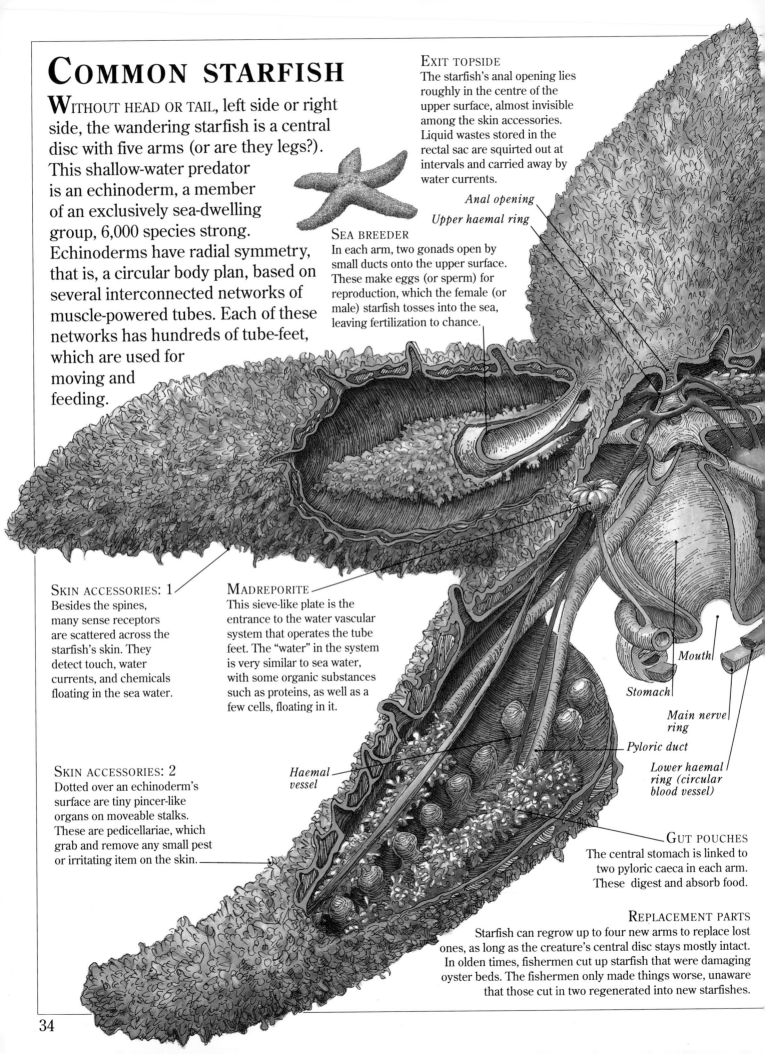

COMMON STARFISH

WITHOUT HEAD OR TAIL, left side or right side, the wandering starfish is a central disc with five arms (or are they legs?). This shallow-water predator is an echinoderm, a member of an exclusively sea-dwelling group, 6,000 species strong. Echinoderms have radial symmetry, that is, a circular body plan, based on several interconnected networks of muscle-powered tubes. Each of these networks has hundreds of tube-feet, which are used for moving and feeding.

EXIT TOPSIDE
The starfish's anal opening lies roughly in the centre of the upper surface, almost invisible among the skin accessories. Liquid wastes stored in the rectal sac are squirted out at intervals and carried away by water currents.

Anal opening

Upper haemal ring

SEA BREEDER
In each arm, two gonads open by small ducts onto the upper surface. These make eggs (or sperm) for reproduction, which the female (or male) starfish tosses into the sea, leaving fertilization to chance.

SKIN ACCESSORIES: 1
Besides the spines, many sense receptors are scattered across the starfish's skin. They detect touch, water currents, and chemicals floating in the sea water.

MADREPORITE
This sieve-like plate is the entrance to the water vascular system that operates the tube feet. The "water" in the system is very similar to sea water, with some organic substances such as proteins, as well as a few cells, floating in it.

SKIN ACCESSORIES: 2
Dotted over an echinoderm's surface are tiny pincer-like organs on moveable stalks. These are pedicellariae, which grab and remove any small pest or irritating item on the skin.

Haemal vessel

Mouth

Stomach

Main nerve ring

Pyloric duct

Lower haemal ring (circular blood vessel)

GUT POUCHES
The central stomach is linked to two pyloric caeca in each arm. These digest and absorb food.

REPLACEMENT PARTS
Starfish can regrow up to four new arms to replace lost ones, as long as the creature's central disc stays mostly intact. In olden times, fishermen cut up starfish that were damaging oyster beds. The fishermen only made things worse, unaware that those cut in two regenerated into new starfishes.

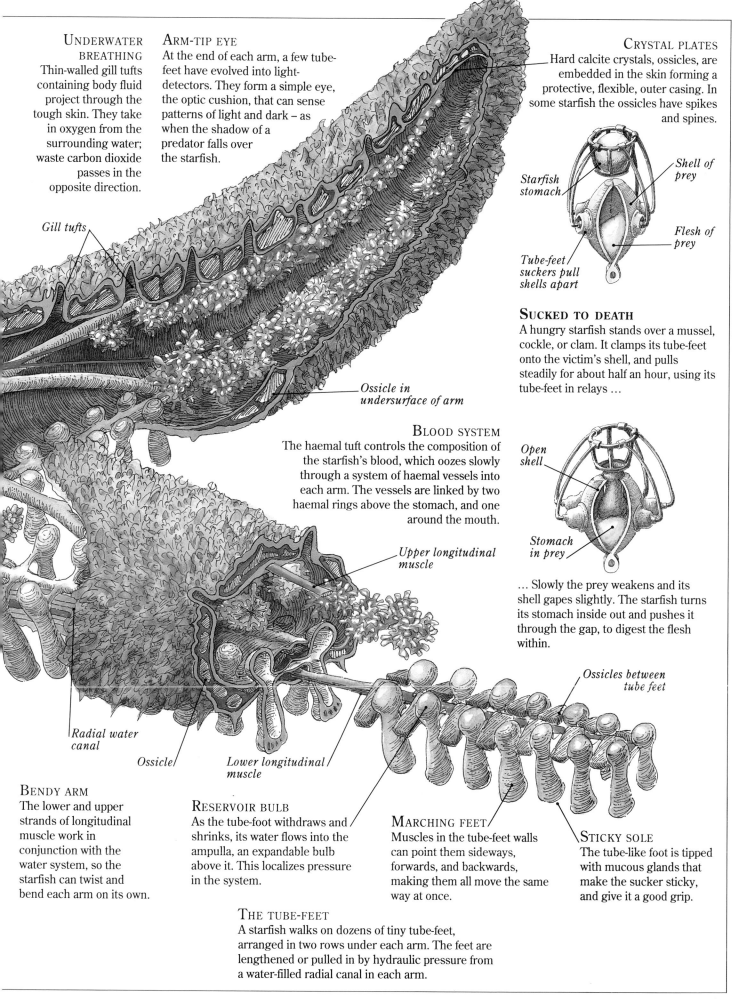

UNDERWATER BREATHING
Thin-walled gill tufts containing body fluid project through the tough skin. They take in oxygen from the surrounding water; waste carbon dioxide passes in the opposite direction.

Gill tufts

ARM-TIP EYE
At the end of each arm, a few tube-feet have evolved into light-detectors. They form a simple eye, the optic cushion, that can sense patterns of light and dark – as when the shadow of a predator falls over the starfish.

CRYSTAL PLATES
Hard calcite crystals, ossicles, are embedded in the skin forming a protective, flexible, outer casing. In some starfish the ossicles have spikes and spines.

Starfish stomach

Shell of prey

Flesh of prey

Tube-feet suckers pull shells apart

SUCKED TO DEATH
A hungry starfish stands over a mussel, cockle, or clam. It clamps its tube-feet onto the victim's shell, and pulls steadily for about half an hour, using its tube-feet in relays …

Ossicle in undersurface of arm

BLOOD SYSTEM
The haemal tuft controls the composition of the starfish's blood, which oozes slowly through a system of haemal vessels into each arm. The vessels are linked by two haemal rings above the stomach, and one around the mouth.

Open shell

Stomach in prey

Upper longitudinal muscle

… Slowly the prey weakens and its shell gapes slightly. The starfish turns its stomach inside out and pushes it through the gap, to digest the flesh within.

Ossicles between tube feet

Radial water canal

Ossicle

Lower longitudinal muscle

BENDY ARM
The lower and upper strands of longitudinal muscle work in conjunction with the water system, so the starfish can twist and bend each arm on its own.

RESERVOIR BULB
As the tube-foot withdraws and shrinks, its water flows into the ampulla, an expandable bulb above it. This localizes pressure in the system.

MARCHING FEET
Muscles in the tube-feet walls can point them sideways, forwards, and backwards, making them all move the same way at once.

STICKY SOLE
The tube-like foot is tipped with mucous glands that make the sucker sticky, and give it a good grip.

THE TUBE-FEET
A starfish walks on dozens of tiny tube-feet, arranged in two rows under each arm. The feet are lengthened or pulled in by hydraulic pressure from a water-filled radial canal in each arm.

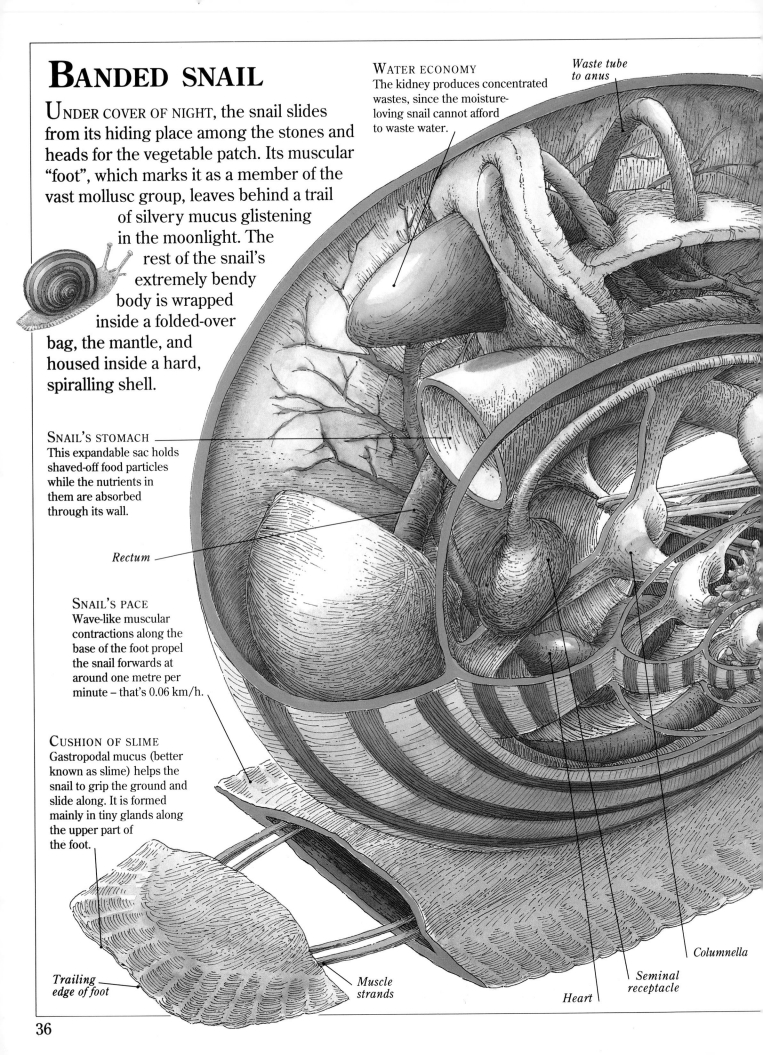

BANDED SNAIL

UNDER COVER OF NIGHT, the snail slides from its hiding place among the stones and heads for the vegetable patch. Its muscular "foot", which marks it as a member of the vast mollusc group, leaves behind a trail of silvery mucus glistening in the moonlight. The rest of the snail's extremely bendy body is wrapped inside a folded-over bag, the mantle, and housed inside a hard, spiralling shell.

WATER ECONOMY
The kidney produces concentrated wastes, since the moisture-loving snail cannot afford to waste water.

Waste tube to anus

SNAIL'S STOMACH
This expandable sac holds shaved-off food particles while the nutrients in them are absorbed through its wall.

Rectum

SNAIL'S PACE
Wave-like muscular contractions along the base of the foot propel the snail forwards at around one metre per minute – that's 0.06 km/h.

CUSHION OF SLIME
Gastropodal mucus (better known as slime) helps the snail to grip the ground and slide along. It is formed mainly in tiny glands along the upper part of the foot.

Trailing edge of foot

Muscle strands

Heart

Seminal receptacle

Columnella

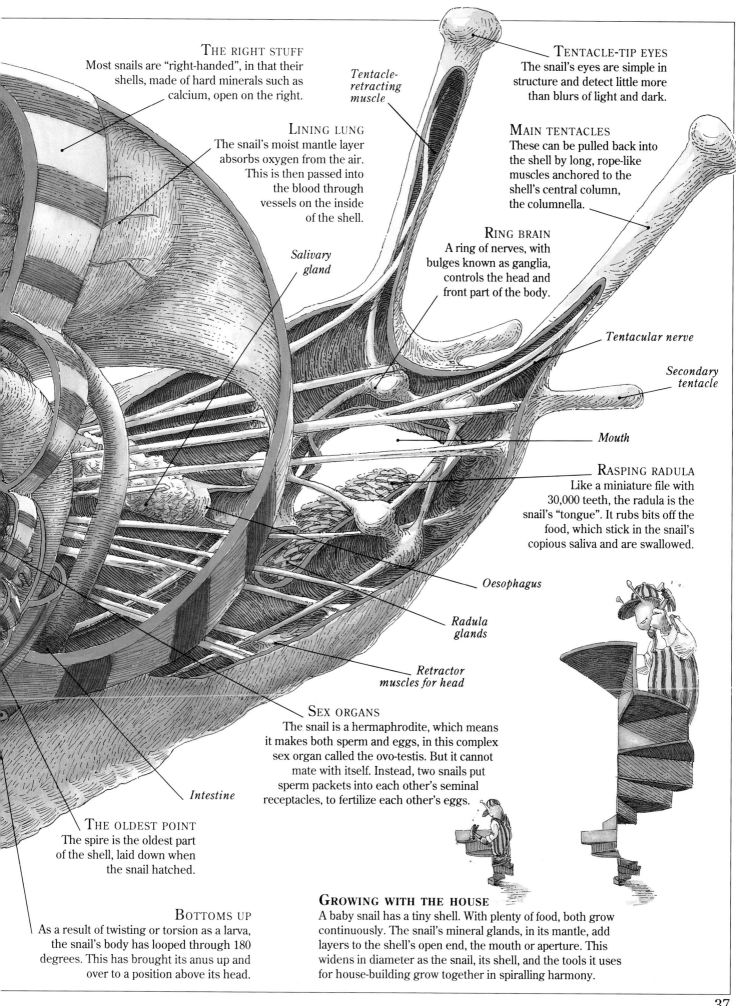

THE RIGHT STUFF
Most snails are "right-handed", in that their shells, made of hard minerals such as calcium, open on the right.

Tentacle-retracting muscle

TENTACLE-TIP EYES
The snail's eyes are simple in structure and detect little more than blurs of light and dark.

LINING LUNG
The snail's moist mantle layer absorbs oxygen from the air. This is then passed into the blood through vessels on the inside of the shell.

MAIN TENTACLES
These can be pulled back into the shell by long, rope-like muscles anchored to the shell's central column, the columnella.

Salivary gland

RING BRAIN
A ring of nerves, with bulges known as ganglia, controls the head and front part of the body.

Tentacular nerve

Secondary tentacle

Mouth

RASPING RADULA
Like a miniature file with 30,000 teeth, the radula is the snail's "tongue". It rubs bits off the food, which stick in the snail's copious saliva and are swallowed.

Oesophagus

Radula glands

Retractor muscles for head

SEX ORGANS
The snail is a hermaphrodite, which means it makes both sperm and eggs, in this complex sex organ called the ovo-testis. But it cannot mate with itself. Instead, two snails put sperm packets into each other's seminal receptacles, to fertilize each other's eggs.

Intestine

THE OLDEST POINT
The spire is the oldest part of the shell, laid down when the snail hatched.

BOTTOMS UP
As a result of twisting or torsion as a larva, the snail's body has looped through 180 degrees. This has brought its anus up and over to a position above its head.

GROWING WITH THE HOUSE
A baby snail has a tiny shell. With plenty of food, both grow continuously. The snail's mineral glands, in its mantle, add layers to the shell's open end, the mouth or aperture. This widens in diameter as the snail, its shell, and the tools it uses for house-building grow together in spiralling harmony.

BLUE-RINGED OCTOPUS

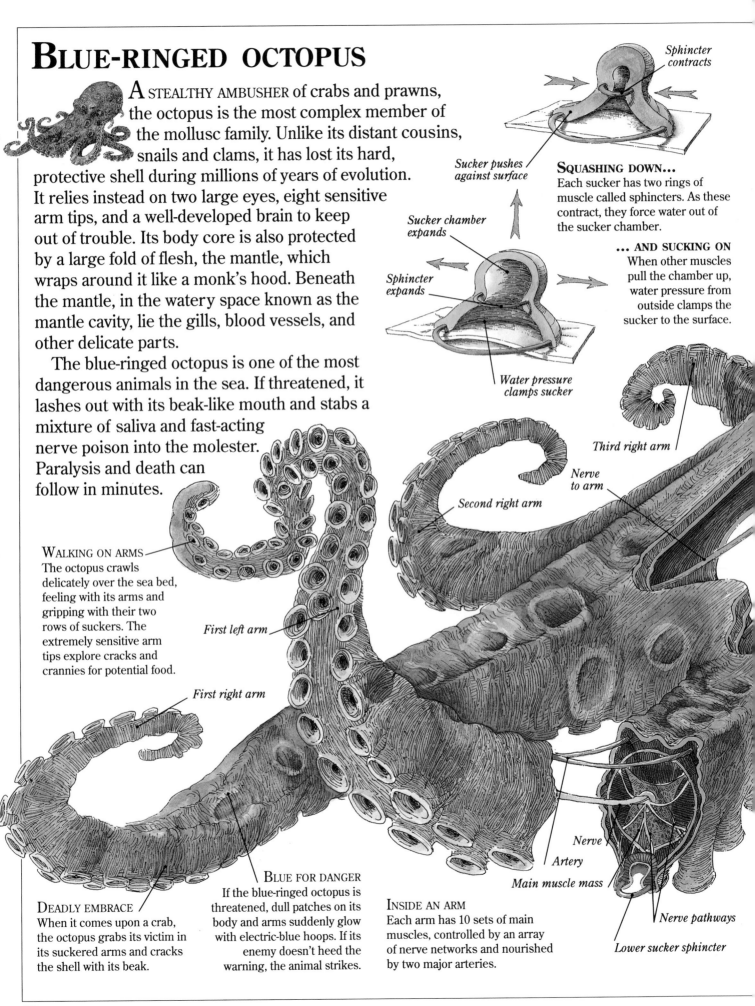

A STEALTHY AMBUSHER of crabs and prawns, the octopus is the most complex member of the mollusc family. Unlike its distant cousins, snails and clams, it has lost its hard, protective shell during millions of years of evolution. It relies instead on two large eyes, eight sensitive arm tips, and a well-developed brain to keep out of trouble. Its body core is also protected by a large fold of flesh, the mantle, which wraps around it like a monk's hood. Beneath the mantle, in the watery space known as the mantle cavity, lie the gills, blood vessels, and other delicate parts.

The blue-ringed octopus is one of the most dangerous animals in the sea. If threatened, it lashes out with its beak-like mouth and stabs a mixture of saliva and fast-acting nerve poison into the molester. Paralysis and death can follow in minutes.

Sphincter contracts

Sucker pushes against surface

SQUASHING DOWN...
Each sucker has two rings of muscle called sphincters. As these contract, they force water out of the sucker chamber.

Sucker chamber expands

Sphincter expands

... AND SUCKING ON
When other muscles pull the chamber up, water pressure from outside clamps the sucker to the surface.

Water pressure clamps sucker

Third right arm

Nerve to arm

Second right arm

WALKING ON ARMS
The octopus crawls delicately over the sea bed, feeling with its arms and gripping with their two rows of suckers. The extremely sensitive arm tips explore cracks and crannies for potential food.

First left arm

First right arm

Nerve

Artery

Main muscle mass

Nerve pathways

Lower sucker sphincter

DEADLY EMBRACE
When it comes upon a crab, the octopus grabs its victim in its suckered arms and cracks the shell with its beak.

BLUE FOR DANGER
If the blue-ringed octopus is threatened, dull patches on its body and arms suddenly glow with electric-blue hoops. If its enemy doesn't heed the warning, the animal strikes.

INSIDE AN ARM
Each arm has 10 sets of main muscles, controlled by an array of nerve networks and nourished by two major arteries.

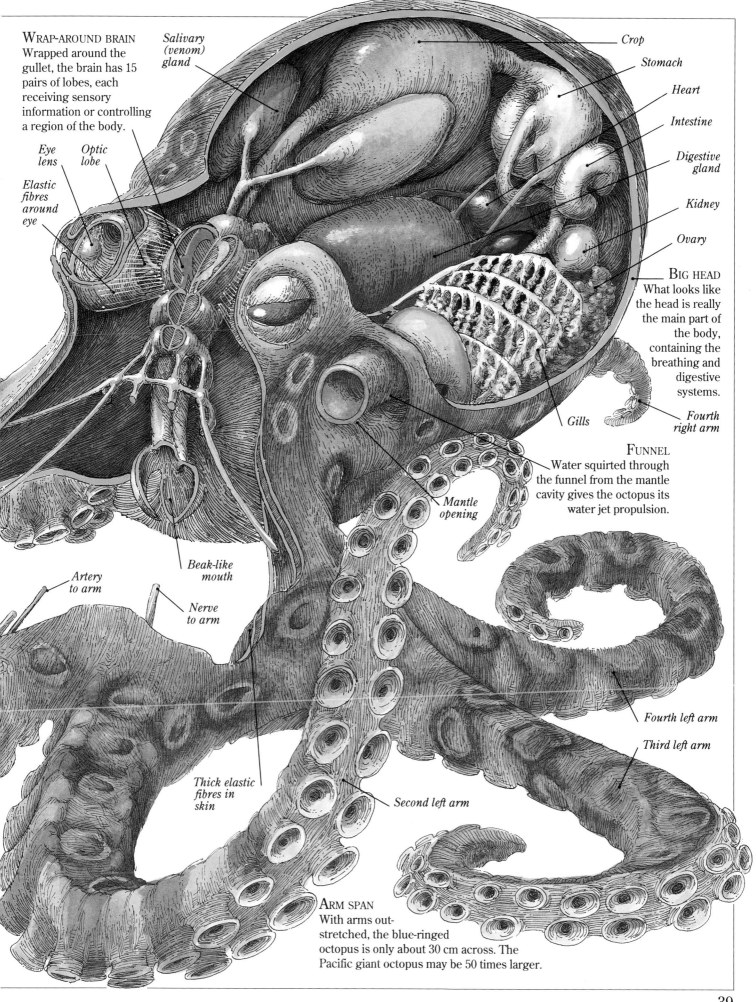

WRAP-AROUND BRAIN
Wrapped around the gullet, the brain has 15 pairs of lobes, each receiving sensory information or controlling a region of the body.

Salivary (venom) gland

Crop

Stomach

Heart

Intestine

Digestive gland

Kidney

Ovary

Eye lens

Optic lobe

Elastic fibres around eye

BIG HEAD
What looks like the head is really the main part of the body, containing the breathing and digestive systems.

Gills

Fourth right arm

FUNNEL
Water squirted through the funnel from the mantle cavity gives the octopus its water jet propulsion.

Mantle opening

Beak-like mouth

Artery to arm

Nerve to arm

Fourth left arm

Third left arm

Thick elastic fibres in skin

Second left arm

ARM SPAN
With arms out-stretched, the blue-ringed octopus is only about 30 cm across. The Pacific giant octopus may be 50 times larger.

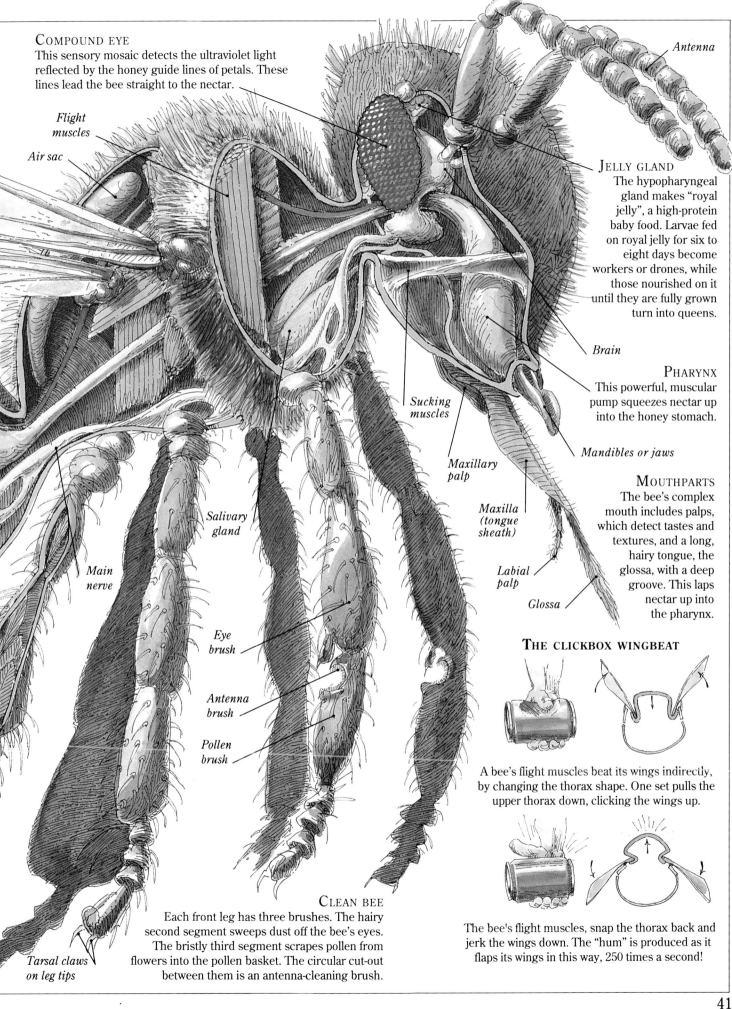

COMPOUND EYE
This sensory mosaic detects the ultraviolet light reflected by the honey guide lines of petals. These lines lead the bee straight to the nectar.

Flight muscles

Air sac

Antenna

JELLY GLAND
The hypopharyngeal gland makes "royal jelly", a high-protein baby food. Larvae fed on royal jelly for six to eight days become workers or drones, while those nourished on it until they are fully grown turn into queens.

Brain

PHARYNX
This powerful, muscular pump squeezes nectar up into the honey stomach.

Mandibles or jaws

MOUTHPARTS
The bee's complex mouth includes palps, which detect tastes and textures, and a long, hairy tongue, the glossa, with a deep groove. This laps nectar up into the pharynx.

Sucking muscles

Maxillary palp

Maxilla (tongue sheath)

Labial palp

Glossa

Salivary gland

Main nerve

Eye brush

Antenna brush

Pollen brush

THE CLICKBOX WINGBEAT

A bee's flight muscles beat its wings indirectly, by changing the thorax shape. One set pulls the upper thorax down, clicking the wings up.

CLEAN BEE
Each front leg has three brushes. The hairy second segment sweeps dust off the bee's eyes. The bristly third segment scrapes pollen from flowers into the pollen basket. The circular cut-out between them is an antenna-cleaning brush.

Tarsal claws on leg tips

The bee's flight muscles, snap the thorax back and jerk the wings down. The "hum" is produced as it flaps its wings in this way, 250 times a second!

MOSQUITO

RIGHT AFTER MATING, the female mosquito goes off in search of a sleeping animal. A tiny prick in the skin, a few minutes sucking, and she flies into the night with a droplet of fresh blood. She has found the proteins to make her eggs – and left you with an itchy red spot.

BZZZZZZZZZZZZZZ
Being a member of the fly family, Diptera, the mosquito has one pair of wings. The female beats hers 400 to 500 times each minute.

Setae (sensitive hairs)

Fringes of scales

Egg sac

Rectum

Egg duct

LEG
Six muscles running down inside each tubular leg bend and straighten the various leg joints.

AIR TUBES
Insects breathe through a network of tubes called tracheae, which open on the skin at tiny holes known as spiracles.

Pouch of gut

Spiracle

MALPIGHIAN ORGANS
Insects and other invertebrates have a system of tiny tubes threading their way around the abdomen. These collect and expel wastes from the internal organs.

BLOOD MEAL
It takes the female mosquito no more than two minutes to suck up a stomachful (about 3 ml) of blood. She then spends three days hiding in a quiet spot, digesting her gory meal.

Setae at joint

LEG JOINTS
The hard body casing, or exoskeleton, is very thin at the joints. This allows the mosquito to bend its legs easily as it walks about in search of a good feeding spot.

FOOT
The tiny foot is equipped with a pair of claws and a tuft of hairs (empodymium) for gripping the smoothest surfaces.

Second tarsal section

First tarsal section

Fifth section of tarsus part of leg

Fourth tarsal section

Third tarsal section

MALARIAL MOSQUITOES
The female *Anopheles* mosquito spreads the deadly disease malaria. As she feeds on an infected person, she takes in the microscopic, disease-causing parasites in the blood. When she "bites" the next person, she injects some saliva and passes on the malaria parasites.

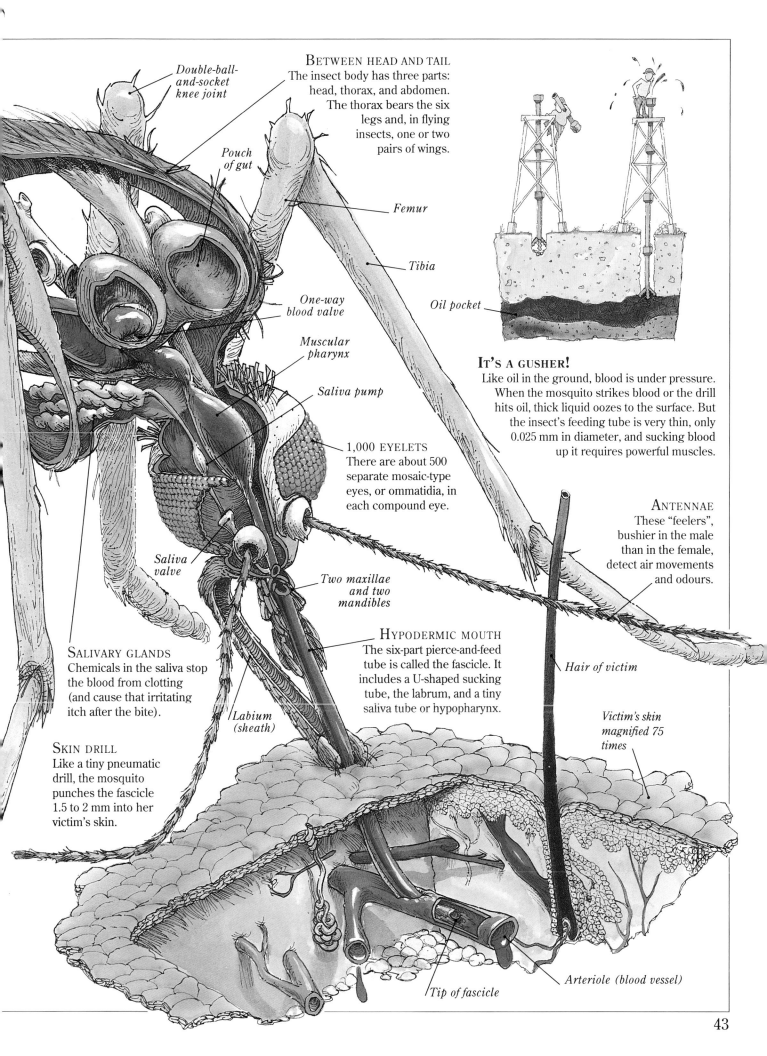

Double-ball-and-socket knee joint

BETWEEN HEAD AND TAIL
The insect body has three parts: head, thorax, and abdomen. The thorax bears the six legs and, in flying insects, one or two pairs of wings.

Pouch of gut

Femur

Tibia

One-way blood valve

Muscular pharynx

Saliva pump

Oil pocket

IT'S A GUSHER!
Like oil in the ground, blood is under pressure. When the mosquito strikes blood or the drill hits oil, thick liquid oozes to the surface. But the insect's feeding tube is very thin, only 0.025 mm in diameter, and sucking blood up it requires powerful muscles.

1,000 EYELETS
There are about 500 separate mosaic-type eyes, or ommatidia, in each compound eye.

ANTENNAE
These "feelers", bushier in the male than in the female, detect air movements and odours.

Saliva valve

Two maxillae and two mandibles

SALIVARY GLANDS
Chemicals in the saliva stop the blood from clotting (and cause that irritating itch after the bite).

Labium (sheath)

HYPODERMIC MOUTH
The six-part pierce-and-feed tube is called the fascicle. It includes a U-shaped sucking tube, the labrum, and a tiny saliva tube or hypopharynx.

Hair of victim

SKIN DRILL
Like a tiny pneumatic drill, the mosquito punches the fascicle 1.5 to 2 mm into her victim's skin.

Victim's skin magnified 75 times

Arteriole (blood vessel)

Tip of fascicle

SPIDER

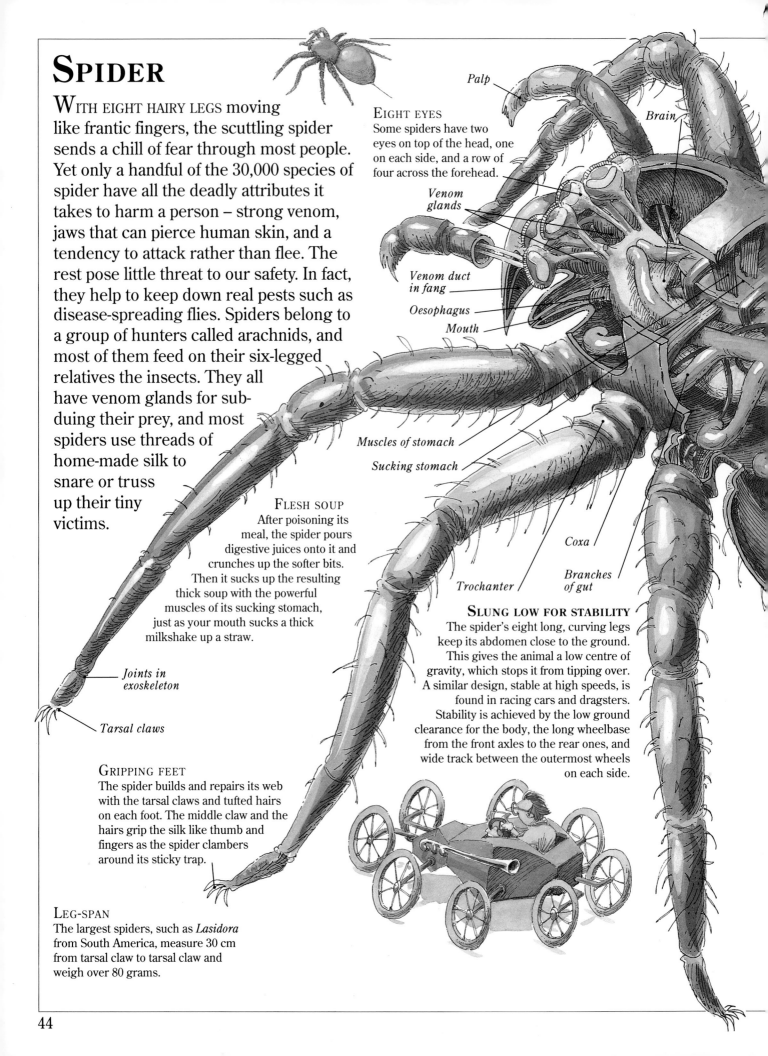

WITH EIGHT HAIRY LEGS moving like frantic fingers, the scuttling spider sends a chill of fear through most people. Yet only a handful of the 30,000 species of spider have all the deadly attributes it takes to harm a person – strong venom, jaws that can pierce human skin, and a tendency to attack rather than flee. The rest pose little threat to our safety. In fact, they help to keep down real pests such as disease-spreading flies. Spiders belong to a group of hunters called arachnids, and most of them feed on their six-legged relatives the insects. They all have venom glands for subduing their prey, and most spiders use threads of home-made silk to snare or truss up their tiny victims.

Palp

Brain

EIGHT EYES
Some spiders have two eyes on top of the head, one on each side, and a row of four across the forehead.

Venom glands

Venom duct in fang

Oesophagus

Mouth

Muscles of stomach

Sucking stomach

FLESH SOUP
After poisoning its meal, the spider pours digestive juices onto it and crunches up the softer bits. Then it sucks up the resulting thick soup with the powerful muscles of its sucking stomach, just as your mouth sucks a thick milkshake up a straw.

Coxa

Branches of gut

Trochanter

SLUNG LOW FOR STABILITY
The spider's eight long, curving legs keep its abdomen close to the ground. This gives the animal a low centre of gravity, which stops it from tipping over. A similar design, stable at high speeds, is found in racing cars and dragsters. Stability is achieved by the low ground clearance for the body, the long wheelbase from the front axles to the rear ones, and wide track between the outermost wheels on each side.

Joints in exoskeleton

Tarsal claws

GRIPPING FEET
The spider builds and repairs its web with the tarsal claws and tufted hairs on each foot. The middle claw and the hairs grip the silk like thumb and fingers as the spider clambers around its sticky trap.

LEG-SPAN
The largest spiders, such as *Lasidora* from South America, measure 30 cm from tarsal claw to tarsal claw and weigh over 80 grams.

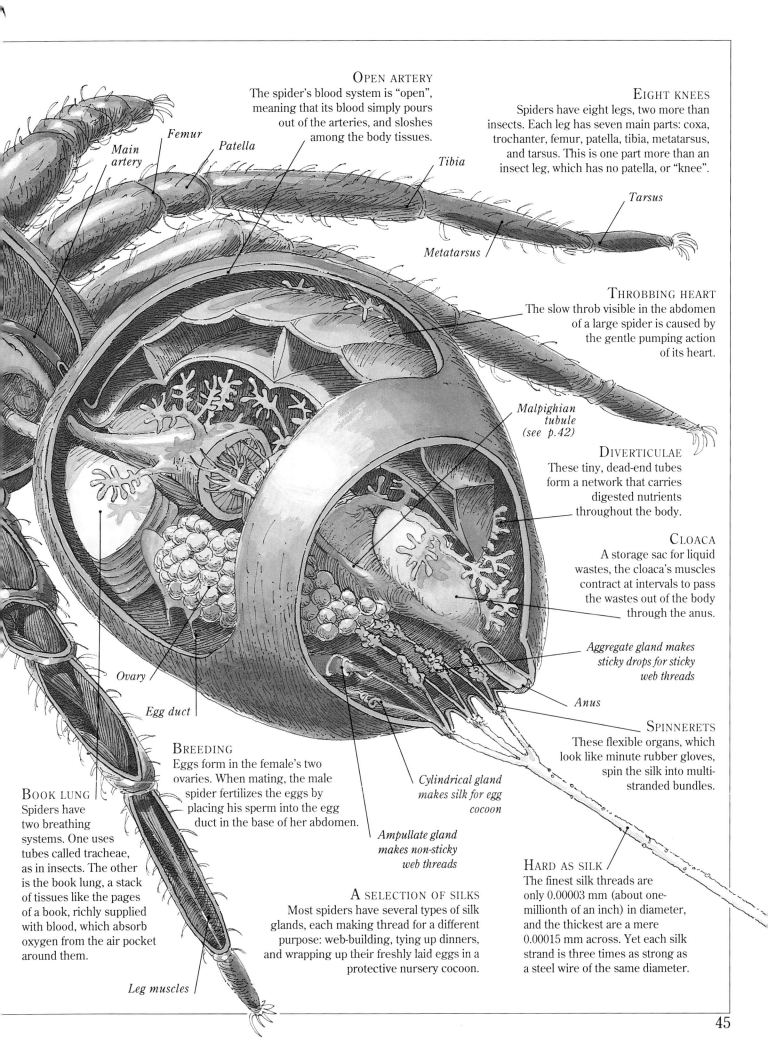

OPEN ARTERY
The spider's blood system is "open", meaning that its blood simply pours out of the arteries, and sloshes among the body tissues.

EIGHT KNEES
Spiders have eight legs, two more than insects. Each leg has seven main parts: coxa, trochanter, femur, patella, tibia, metatarsus, and tarsus. This is one part more than an insect leg, which has no patella, or "knee".

Main artery

Femur

Patella

Tibia

Tarsus

Metatarsus

THROBBING HEART
The slow throb visible in the abdomen of a large spider is caused by the gentle pumping action of its heart.

Malpighian tubule (see p.42)(see p.42)

DIVERTICULAE
These tiny, dead-end tubes form a network that carries digested nutrients throughout the body.

CLOACA
A storage sac for liquid wastes, the cloaca's muscles contract at intervals to pass the wastes out of the body through the anus.

Aggregate gland makes sticky drops for sticky web threads

Anus

SPINNERETS
These flexible organs, which look like minute rubber gloves, spin the silk into multi-stranded bundles.

Ovary

Egg duct

BREEDING
Eggs form in the female's two ovaries. When mating, the male spider fertilizes the eggs by placing his sperm into the egg duct in the base of her abdomen.

Cylindrical gland makes silk for egg cocoon

Ampullate gland makes non-sticky web threads

BOOK LUNG
Spiders have two breathing systems. One uses tubes called tracheae, as in insects. The other is the book lung, a stack of tissues like the pages of a book, richly supplied with blood, which absorb oxygen from the air pocket around them.

Leg muscles

A SELECTION OF SILKS
Most spiders have several types of silk glands, each making thread for a different purpose: web-building, tying up dinners, and wrapping up their freshly laid eggs in a protective nursery cocoon.

HARD AS SILK
The finest silk threads are only 0.00003 mm (about one-millionth of an inch) in diameter, and the thickest are a mere 0.00015 mm across. Yet each silk strand is three times as strong as a steel wire of the same diameter.

45

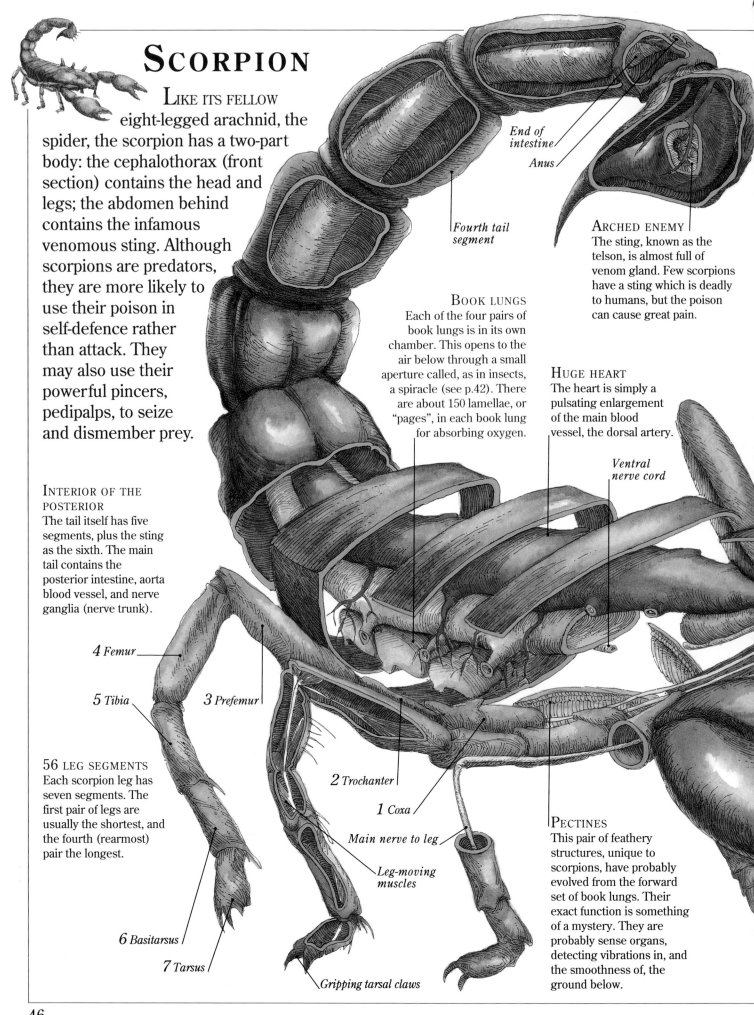

SCORPION

LIKE ITS FELLOW eight-legged arachnid, the spider, the scorpion has a two-part body: the cephalothorax (front section) contains the head and legs; the abdomen behind contains the infamous venomous sting. Although scorpions are predators, they are more likely to use their poison in self-defence rather than attack. They may also use their powerful pincers, pedipalps, to seize and dismember prey.

INTERIOR OF THE POSTERIOR
The tail itself has five segments, plus the sting as the sixth. The main tail contains the posterior intestine, aorta blood vessel, and nerve ganglia (nerve trunk).

4 Femur

5 Tibia

3 Prefemur

56 LEG SEGMENTS
Each scorpion leg has seven segments. The first pair of legs are usually the shortest, and the fourth (rearmost) pair the longest.

6 Basitarsus

7 Tarsus

End of intestine

Anus

Fourth tail segment

ARCHED ENEMY
The sting, known as the telson, is almost full of venom gland. Few scorpions have a sting which is deadly to humans, but the poison can cause great pain.

BOOK LUNGS
Each of the four pairs of book lungs is in its own chamber. This opens to the air below through a small aperture called, as in insects, a spiracle (see p.42). There are about 150 lamellae, or "pages", in each book lung for absorbing oxygen.

HUGE HEART
The heart is simply a pulsating enlargement of the main blood vessel, the dorsal artery.

Ventral nerve cord

2 Trochanter

1 Coxa

Main nerve to leg

Leg-moving muscles

PECTINES
This pair of feathery structures, unique to scorpions, have probably evolved from the forward set of book lungs. Their exact function is something of a mystery. They are probably sense organs, detecting vibrations in, and the smoothness of, the ground below.

Gripping tarsal claws

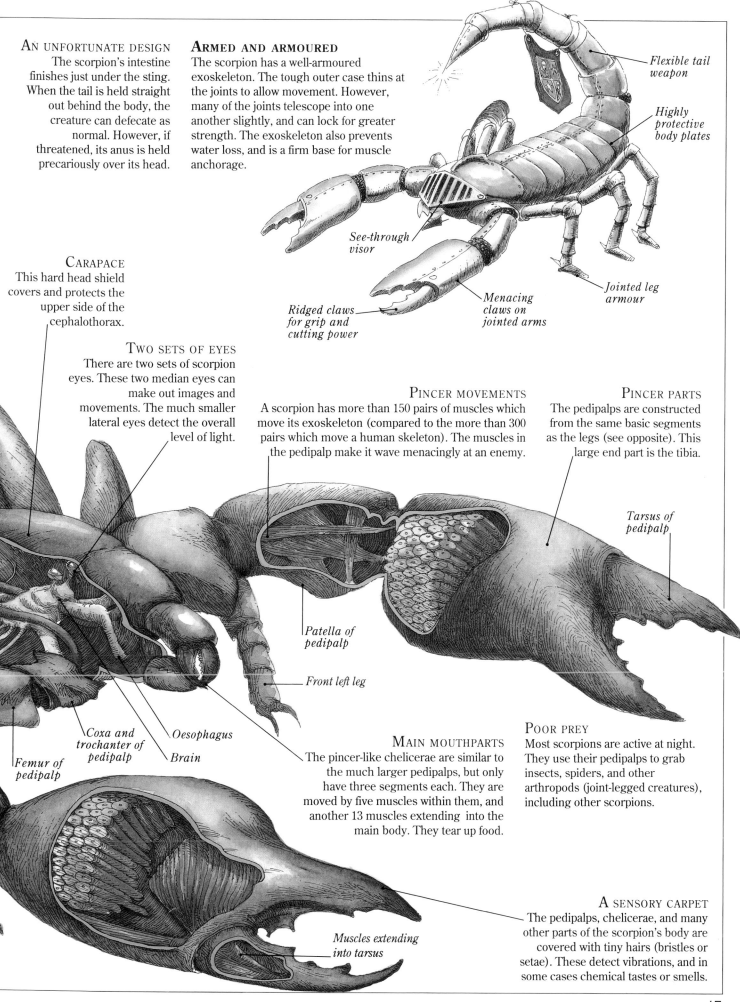

AN UNFORTUNATE DESIGN
The scorpion's intestine finishes just under the sting. When the tail is held straight out behind the body, the creature can defecate as normal. However, if threatened, its anus is held precariously over its head.

ARMED AND ARMOURED
The scorpion has a well-armoured exoskeleton. The tough outer case thins at the joints to allow movement. However, many of the joints telescope into one another slightly, and can lock for greater strength. The exoskeleton also prevents water loss, and is a firm base for muscle anchorage.

Flexible tail weapon

Highly protective body plates

See-through visor

Ridged claws for grip and cutting power

Menacing claws on jointed arms

Jointed leg armour

CARAPACE
This hard head shield covers and protects the upper side of the cephalothorax.

TWO SETS OF EYES
There are two sets of scorpion eyes. These two median eyes can make out images and movements. The much smaller lateral eyes detect the overall level of light.

PINCER MOVEMENTS
A scorpion has more than 150 pairs of muscles which move its exoskeleton (compared to the more than 300 pairs which move a human skeleton). The muscles in the pedipalp make it wave menacingly at an enemy.

PINCER PARTS
The pedipalps are constructed from the same basic segments as the legs (see opposite). This large end part is the tibia.

Tarsus of pedipalp

Patella of pedipalp

Front left leg

Coxa and trochanter of pedipalp

Oesophagus

Brain

Femur of pedipalp

MAIN MOUTHPARTS
The pincer-like chelicerae are similar to the much larger pedipalps, but only have three segments each. They are moved by five muscles within them, and another 13 muscles extending into the main body. They tear up food.

POOR PREY
Most scorpions are active at night. They use their pedipalps to grab insects, spiders, and other arthropods (joint-legged creatures), including other scorpions.

Muscles extending into tarsus

A SENSORY CARPET
The pedipalps, chelicerae, and many other parts of the scorpion's body are covered with tiny hairs (bristles or setae). These detect vibrations, and in some cases chemical tastes or smells.

47

INDEX

A
ankle bones, *see* tarsals
anus: bee 40, elephant 12, frog 30, scorpion 47, snail 36, 37, spider 45, starfish 34

B
backbones, *see* vertebrae
bat, brown 14-15
bee 40-41
bladder: elephant 12, tortoise, triceratops 29
blood: bee 40, octopus 38, snail 37, spider 45, starfish 35
brain: bat 14, bee 41, crocodile 26, frog 31, gorilla 9, octopus 38, 39, scorpion 47, shark 33, snail 37, spider 44, whale 6
breastbone, *see* sternum

C
camel, dromedary 10-11
carpals: bat 14, chicken 21, gorilla 9, owl 18, tortoise 24
cervical vertebrae, *see* neck
chicken 10-11
clavicle: bat 14, chicken 21, tortoise 25
crocodile 26-27

E
ears: bat 14, crocodile 26, elephant 13, frog 31, kangaroo 17, owl 18, tortoise 24
egg, chicken 20, 21, frog 30, mosquito 42, snail 37, spider 45, starfish 34
elephant, african 12-13
epidermis, *see* skin
eyes: bee 41, crocodile 26, frog 31, mosquito 43, octopus 38, 39, owl 18, scorpion 47, shark 33, snail 37, snake 22, spider 44, starfish 35

F
femur: bat 15, camel 11, chicken 20, crocodile 27, elephant 12, frog 30, gorilla 8, kangaroo 16, mosquito 43, owl 19, scorpion 46, 47, spider 45, tortoise 25, triceratops 29
fibula: camel 11, crocodile 27, gorilla 8, triceratops 29
fingers, *see* phalanges
foot, *see* metatarsals
forearm bone, *see* radius, ulna
frog 30-31

G
gills: octopus 38, 39, shark 33, starfish 35
gorilla, mountain 8-9
gullet, *see* oesophagus
gut, *see* intestines

H
heart: bee 40, camel 11, crocodile 27, elephant 13, frog 31, octopus 39, scorpion 46, shark 33, snail 36, snake 22, spider 45, triceratops 29
hip, *see* pelvis
humerus: bat 14, camel 11, chicken 20, crocodile 27, elephant 13, gorilla 9, owl 18, tortoise 24

I – J
intestines: bat 15, bee 40, camel 11, chicken 20, crocodile 27, elephant 12, frog 31, octopus 39, owl 19, scorpion 46, 47, shark 33, snail 39, snake 22, 23, tortoise 25, triceratops 29, whale 7
jaw, *see* mandible

K
kangaroo 16-17
kidneys: bat 15, crocodile 27, elephant 12, frog 30, octopus 39, shark 32, snail 36, snake 22, 23, whale 7
knee: bat 15, camel 11, crocodile 27, frog 31, kangaroo 16, mosquito 43, owl 19, spider 45, triceratops 29

L
liver: crocodile 27, snake 22, triceratops 29, whale 7
lungs: bat 15, camel 11, chicken 20, crocodile 27, elephant 12, frog 30, 31, owl 18, 19, scorpion 46, snake 22, 23, spider 45, tortoise 25, triceratops 29, whale 6

M
mammary glands: camel 11, kangaroo 16, 17
mandible: bat 14, bee 41, camel 10, crocodile 26, kangaroo 17, mosquito 43, owl 18, shark 33, snake 22, 23, spider 44, tortoise 24, triceratops 28, 29, whale 6
metatarsals: camel 11, chicken 20, gorilla 8, owl 19, spider 45
mosquito 42-43

N
neck: camel 10, chicken 21, crocodile 26, human 9, gorilla 9, owl 18, tortoise 24

nostril: bat 14, crocodile 26, elephant 13, kangaroo 17, shark 33, tortoise 24, triceratops 28, whale 6

O
octopus 38-39
oesophagus: bat 14, camel 11, chicken 21, crocodile 27, kangaroo 17, octopus 39, owl 18, scorpion 47, shark 32, snail 37, snake 22, spider 44, tortoise 24, triceratops 28
ovaries: chicken 20, elephant 12, gorilla 8, octopus 39, spider 45
ovum, *see* egg
owl, eagle 18-19

P
patella, *see* knee
pelvis: bat 15, camel 11, chicken 20, crocodile 27, elephant 12, frog 30, gorilla 8, kangaroo 16, tortoise 25, triceratops 29, whale 7
phalanges: bat 15, camel 11, chicken 20, crocodile 27, elephant 12, 13, frog 31, gorilla 8, kangaroo 17, triceratops 28, 29, whale 7

R
radius: bat 14, camel 11, chicken 21, gorilla 9, owl 18, tortoise 24, triceratops 28
rattlesnake 22-23
ribs: bat 15, chicken 21, crocodile 27, elephant 13, gorilla 8, kangaroo 16, tortoise 25, triceratops 29, whale 7

S
salivary glands: bee 41, camel 10, mosquito 42, 43, octopus 39, snail 37
scapula: camel 11, crocodile 27, frog 31, kangaroo 17, tortoise 24, 25
scorpion 46-47
shark, great white 32-33
shin bone, *see* fibula, tibia
shoulder bone, *see* scapula
skin: crocodile 27, elephant 12, 13, frog 30, octopus 39, shark 32, snake, 22, 23, starfish 34, 35, tortoise 24, triceratops 28
skull: bat 14, camel 10, crocodile 26, gorilla 9, kangaroo 17, triceratops 28, whale 6
snail 36-37
spider 44-45
spinal cord: bat 14, frog 31, shark 32, snake 22, tortoise 24

spiracles: bee 40, mosquito 42, scorpion 46, shark 33
starfish 34-35
sternum: chicken 21, elephant 13
sting: bee 40, scorpion 46
stomach: bee 40, camel 10, 11, crocodile 27, elephant 12, frog 31, gorilla 8, kangaroo 16, octopus 39, owl 19, snail 36, snake 22, spider 44, starfish 34, 35, triceratops 28, 29, whale 7

T
tail: bat 15, chicken 20, crocodile 26, 27, elephant 12, kangaroo 16, owl 19, scorpion 46, 47, shark 32, snake 23, tortoise 25, triceratops 29, whale 7
tarsals: bat 15, camel 11, chicken 20, elephant 12, frog 30
tarsus: mosquito 42, scorpion 46, 47, spider 44, 45
teeth: bat 14, 15, crocodile 26, elephant 13, gorilla 9, shark 33, snake 22, triceratops 28
testes: shark 32, snail 37, snake 23, whale 7
thigh bone, *see* femur
tibia: bat 15, camel 11, chicken 20, crocodile 27, frog 30, gorilla 8, mosquito 43, owl 19, scorpion 46, 47, spider 45, triceratops 29
toes, *see* phalanges
tongue: frog 31, snail 37, tortoise 24, whale 6, 7
tortoise, giant 24-25
trachea: bat 14, camel 10, chicken 21, crocodile 27, elephant 13, kangaroo 17, mosquito 42, owl 18, snake 22, 23, spider 45, tortoise 24, triceratops 28
triceratops 28-29

U
ulna: camel 11, chicken 21, elephant 12, gorilla 9, owl 18, tortoise 24, triceratops 28
uterus: chicken 20, 21, elephant 12, gorilla 8, kangaroo 16, 17

V
vertebrae: camel 10, 11, crocodile 27, gorilla 8, frog 30, human 9, kangaroo 16, snake 22, shark 32, tortoise 24, triceratops 29

W
whale, blue 6-7
windpipe, *see* trachea
wings: bat 14, 15, bee 40, 41, insect 43, mosquito 42, owl 18
womb, *see* uterus

ACKNOWLEDGMENTS

The illustrator and author would like to thank:
• James Kirkwood, Head Veterinary Scientist at Regent's Park Zoo, London
• The staff of the Zoology Library of the Natural History Museum, London

• The staff of the Wolfson Library of the Zoological Society, London
• The Cob Breeding Company, Chelmsford, Essex, and Sovereign Chicken Ltd, Eye, Suffolk
• The countless anatomists over the centuries, whose endless pulling, poking and prodding

around inside every creature under the sun, has provided the raw material for this book

Dorling Kindersley would like to thank:
• Sophie Mitchell, Colin Walton, Manisha Patel, and Meriel Yates for editorial and design guidance